CAVALIER KING CHARLES SPANIELS TODAY

SHEILA SMITH

HOWELL
BOOK HOUSE

NEW YORK

HOWELL BOOK HOUSE
A Simon & Schuster Macmillan company,
1633 Broadway, New York, NY 10019.

MACMILLAN is a registered trademark of Macmillan, Inc.

Library of Congress Cataloging-in-Publication data

Smith, Sheila, 1944–
  Cavalier King Charles Spaniels today / Sheila Smith

    p.   cm.
  ISBN 0-87605-093-3
  1. Cavalier King Charles spaniels.   I. Title
  SF429.C36S59   1995   95-7585
  636.7'3 – dc20   CIP

10 9 8 7 6 5 4 3
Printed and bound in Singapore

CONTENTS

Chapter One: INTRODUCING THE CAVALIER   6

The versatile Cavalier; The fearless Cavalier; Royal connections; The Cavalier colours; The breed's outstanding feature; Looking at Cavaliers; Good breeding; The ethics of the breed.

Chapter Two: PICKING PUPPIES   18

'Lucky' markings; Omens; The scientific approach; Examining conformation; Checking teeth formation; Assessing the markings; The ideal puppy; Difficult assessment areas.

Chapter Three: CARING FOR YOUR CAVALIER   27

The technical side; Arriving home; Following the breeder's instructions; Managing the new puppy; Lead training; Basic training; Grooming the new puppy; Detailed grooming.

Chapter Four: THE BREED STANDARD   41

The British Breed Standard; The American Breed Standard; Analysis of the standards.

Chapter Five: THE EARLY BREEDERS   58

The Cavalier catalyst; Amice Pitt: Ttiweh line; Getting established; Starting again; Mrs Jennings' Plantation line; Some prominent Post-war lines; Barbara Keswick's Pargeter line; Breeders of the fifties and sixties; Littlebreach and Chacombe lines; The start of the Salador line.

Chapter Six: A DOG OF DOGS   74

Rose Mullion; Ch. Homaranne Caption; Susan Burgess: Crisdigs Line; Pamela Turle: Sunninghill; Salador Charlock; The golden years; The Coakers: Homerbrent and Homaranne; Allan Hall and John Evans: Alansmere; The Thornhills: Kindrum; The Frys: Amantras; My own Saladors; Breeding in the 1990s.

Chapter Seven: THE CAVALIER IN NORTH AMERICA   91

The early history; The judging system; The championship point system; Championship awards; The breeders; Jo Ann Carvill: BJ Cavaliers; Gammon and Schroll: Ravenrush; Barbara Garnett Smith: Laughing Cavaliers; Canadian connections; Robbi Jones: Rutherford Cavaliers; A great champion; Brigida Reynolds: Mostyn Cavaliers; Ann Robins: Chadwick Cavaliers; Thaeder: Redthea Cavaliers; Summary.

Chapter Eight: THE INTERNATIONAL SCENE   **102**
Europe; Scandinavia; Australia and New Zealand; Ireland.

Chapter Nine: WHOLE COLOURS   **109**
The poor relations; Growing interest; Ch. Caderyn Black Tulip and family; Joan
Pagan's Soratas and descendants; The change in fortunes; The future.

Chapter Ten: KEEPING THINGS SIMPLE   **122**
Traditions; Using common sense; Breed type; Judging; Exhibiting; Successful
breeders.

Chapter Eleven: BREEDING CAVALIERS   **126**
The brood bitch – written and unwritten rules; The ideal subject; Early
preparation; The signs of pregnancy; Feeding the pregnant bitch; Exercise; The
vet; Preparing for the whelping; The whelping; When things go wrong; Reviving
'dead' puppies.

Chapter Twelve: REARING A LITTER   **139**
The first days; The first few weeks; Puppy abnormalities; Natural Rearing;
Feeding puppies; Adult diets; Outside runs.

Chapter Thirteen: HEALTH CARE   **147**
Pills and potions; Abscesses; Anal glands; Burns and scalds; Colitis and Parvo-
virus: Emergency treatment for colitis; Constipation; Cut feet and torn out nails;
Depraved appetite; Diarrhoea; Ear canker; Foul breath; Fractures, dislocations and
sprains; Heart trouble; Heat stroke; Hernias; Kennel cough; Lack of appetite;
Mastitis; Poisons; Pyometra; Rheumatism and arthritis; Ringworm; Skin and coat
problems; Sore eyes; Stings; Tumours; Warts; Worms; Reassurance.

APPENDIX   **159**

*I would like to dedicate this book to the
Cavaliers and their breeders who really gave
my life a whole new dimension.*

ACKNOWLEDGMENTS

My thanks to Julie Roberts for her line drawings, to Margaret Adamson for her grooming and equipment photos, and to Jane Bowdler for the loan of the books and papers belonging to her late mother, Amice Pitt.

Sheila Smith.

*Salador Charlock:
Sire of four English
Champions, five
overseas
Champions, and
Dog World Top
Cavalier Stud 1986.*

*Photo:
Diane Pearce.*

Chapter One

INTRODUCING THE CAVALIER

THE VERSATILE CAVALIER

The Cavalier King Charles Spaniel belongs to the Toy Group of dogs, and is not only the largest-sized variety but usually has the highest number of breed entries at the Championship shows and in the Breed registrations, even more than the very popular Yorkshire Terrier.

The early breeders could never have imagined, or foreseen, how much the Cavalier would excel in top flight competition with all breeds, or how they would enjoy such great popularity as pets, because those pioneers had difficulty in getting someone in authority to take their endeavours seriously, let alone obtaining breed registrations.

Over the years the sporting, affectionate and devoted nature of the Cavalier King Charles Spaniel has endeared the breed to many people all over the world from all walks of life. Their general appearance gives them versatility when it comes to ownership, for although they are a Toy dog, their sporting and active appearance makes them look perfectly in place walking with the most masculine gentleman. Yet their elegant, aristocratic air and their choice of glamorous coloured silky coats blend in with the fashionable lady owner shopping down the most sophisticated streets in a city.

Their small, handy size and non-trim silky coats make the breed ideal house dogs. Delightfully gentle with the youngest child and the most elderly adults, the Cavalier King Charles Spaniel can be trusted implicitly not to show temper, even when accidentally hurt. The breed's likely reaction is to yelp and run away for refuge rather than to retaliate. So breeders must, for the puppy's sake, make every endeavour to ensure that, when placing their puppies in new homes, they only go to where well-behaved children live.

The Cavalier is a highly adaptable dog, eager to join in with any activity, be it a car ride to the shops, a sponsored walk, or just pottering about in the garden with their owner. Their undemanding nature makes them very easy to live with, especially if the owner is not up to taking them for a walk every day. They are quite happy to play in the garden, unlike, say, a Labrador Retriever dog, where the owner hardly dare jingle the collar and chain for fear of being pestered! But, taken on the longest hike, the Cavalier can keep up and out-stay the best of them.

Usually biddable, and highly intelligent, the Cavalier can be trained to high standards of obedience work, and this aspect of the breed is much in evidence particularly in the USA

Ch. Spring Tide at Alansmere. The Cavalier's loving and affectionate nature has made the breed a favourite worldwide.

Photo: T. Morgan.

Laughing Lord Woodstock exploring the snow in the USA. Owned by Mrs Benjamin R. Field III. A natural joie de vivre is a hallmark of the breed.

The Harmonic Cavaliers take the plunge in Finland. Owned by Mrs Heli Anneli Vare. Cavaliers are highly adaptable, and they are ready to join in all activities.

The perfect companion dog: Julie Roberts with her beloved pets, Candy and Tansy.

Photo: Bernard Mitchell.

and Canada where even show champions carry Obedience Titles. But to my mind, once one really gets to know the breed and understand what motivates the dog, the Cavalier is not really suited to boring drill work, and is unlike a breed such as the brilliant Border Collie, who absolutely revels in this type of activity. To me it seems to be such a pity to waste the Cavalier's joie de vivre on what they consider to be a mundane activity.

Although a Toy breed, the Cavalier is far from being fragile and delicate and is indeed usually a very robust, healthy and hardy little dog, able to exist quite happily in outdoor accommodation in a country with a mild climate all year round. They love to swim and run in freedom, and even the deepest snowfall fails to suppress their exuberance and love of the great outdoors. To deprive the Cavalier of daily fresh air and free running is to be very unkind and misguided. Cavaliers particularly yearn for human companionship. If there are not too many of them in one place, the dogs should be allowed to live partly or wholly in the home of their owner, where as a breed they are best enjoyed.

The breed has a certain element of endearment which is difficult to comprehend until you have every actually owned one, and I can only liken them to eating a packet of crisps – it is very difficult to stop at one! Even the smallest Cavalier puppy at a few weeks old is astonishingly bright and intelligent, listening to every word one says; a more sober and endearing little being would be difficult to find. When picked up level with the face so the eyes roll round to look at you, the expression is enough for one to want to borrow them for a life-time. No-one would ever guess that such a demure and solemn little creature could eventually end up travelling through life with such gay abandon and disregard for danger.

THE FEARLESS CAVALIER

The characteristic temperament of the typical Cavalier King Charles Spaniel is 'gay and fearless' and so the dog can also be completely oblivious to danger. They can so easily fall foul of an intolerant larger dog, as the breed have no fear. The Cavalier thinks that they are everybody's friend and they can spontaneously fawn around the large dog's head and front legs. These innocent actions on the part of the Cavalier can lead to dire consequences unless they are checked by their owner or handler.

The Cavalier's road traffic sense is virtually non-existent and, as a breed, they are completely unperturbed, when standing in the middle of the road, to see a ten-ton tipper lorry bearing down on them. No Cavalier owner should ever attempt, and should certainly never show off their dog performing the 'walk at heel' without a leash on a public highway or footpath or, for that matter, use the popular Flexi lead unless positive that the locking mechanism is engaged securely. A proper leather or chain lead with a strong clip is the safest, attached to a fitted chain or leather collar that is impossible to pull over the dog's head, even in an emergency. The Flexi lead is an excellent invention when used in the proper way and is invaluable for exercise on open ground, enabling the dog to run and cover a large area without actually being released from its handler.

The reason for these innocent shortcomings in the Cavalier King Charles Spaniel's character is that the breed finds it difficult to concentrate for any length of time, being so full of mischief and insatiably inquisitive, so that the dog's attention is very easily diverted by unexpected attractions. Without any warning at all the Cavalier is quite likely to dash across the road in front of oncoming traffic and, as is recorded in this book, even some famous Cavaliers of the past did not avoid these tragic consequences. Therefore the Cavalier's 'gay and fearless' nature, tolerance of unsympathetic, perhaps cruel handling, and blindness to danger can all be detrimental, so owners must constantly think ahead and be prepared to take care of life for them. Cavaliers' sporting nature makes them an ideal country companion, and they would even make excellent gun dogs but for the fact that, after stylishly quartering the ground and having the ability to pick up small game to retrieve to the handler, their attention is so easily diverted on the way back, perhaps by an interesting smell on the ground!

Cavaliers would make wonderful guard dogs, with their astuteness and keen hearing which triggers off their enthusiastic barking – were it not for their deep love of human beings, good or bad, their easily diverted attention and their keen interest in the instantaneous. With wagging tail the Cavalier is not only likely to welcome the burglars into the home, but also with twinkling eyes and panting tongue accompany the robbers to where the silver is kept.

ROYAL CONNECTIONS

The Cavalier King Charles Spaniel was first established as a separate breed by a small group of breeders in 1928, but it was only in 1948 that the first Champion was made up after the Kennel Club had recognised the breed in the intervening years.

Hundreds of years before this, the popular painters of their day, particularly in the 15th Century, give much visual evidence of the presence of the Cavalier's ancestors, the Toy Spaniels and King Charles Spaniels.

At some time in their life most people have wandered into the palaces, ancestral homes, art galleries and museums which exist all over the world and gazed up at the beautiful oil paintings from that period. Many show the fine-muzzled, small spaniel-type dog depicted in the situations that their descendants so often enjoy today. The toy dogs, mostly seen as silky-haired particolours, are observed in rural hunting pictures, playing around the skirts of their aristocratic owners with their children, or sharing the home domestic scene. The Toy spaniels were very popular with the ladies of the court and it is not very difficult to deduce how the little dogs came by the nickname 'Comforters'. The ladies' pets not only served as loving companions. Their owners could also keep warm in the huge draughty houses by nursing the dogs in their laps and retiring to their beds with them.

These days the Cavalier brings untold pleasure into the lives of innumerable men, women and children from all walks of life, but the evidence of their companionable associations with Royalty and the aristocracy is vast – none more so than with King Charles II from whence the original Toy dogs took their name, and the little spaniels were often painted with their royal owner and accompanied him everywhere. The dogs became so much a part of his life that the King, according to legend, issued a Royal Edict that no King Charles Spaniel be denied entry to any public place, including theatres.

King Charles appeared, according to documents of the day, to be a terribly engrossed breeder of these little dogs. As the diarist John Evelyn noted in his entry on February 4th 1685: "He tooke delight in having a number of little spaniels follow him and lie in his bedchamber, where he often suffer'd the bitches to puppy and give suck, which render'd it very offensive, and indeede made the whole Court nasty and stinking."

The King apparently found it difficult to combine his canine interests with his kingly duties, for another diarist, Samuel Pepys, blamed him for "playing with his dogs all the while, and not minding his business". But by endeavouring to keep up with his Royal activities, King Charles's attentions were often diverted and he appeared to be always losing a dog or two as well. His concern for their safety was often displayed in his urgent appeals for them to be found and returned.

One advertisement which appeared in the Mercurius Publicus between June 28 and July 5 1660, probably written by King Charles himself, read as follows: "We must call upon you again for a Black dog between a greyhound and a spaniel, no white about him, only a streak

Children of Charles I, painted by Van Dyck (1599-1641). This was one of the paintings used to determine the new Breed Standard.

In the collection of the Earl of Pembroke at Wilton House, Salisbury.

on his brest, and his tayl a little bobbed. It was His Majesties own Dog, and doubtless was stoln, for the dog was not born nor bred in England, and would not forsake His master. Whosoever findes him may acquaint any at Whitehal for the Dog was better known at Court, than those who stole him. Will they never leave robbing his Majesty! Must he not keep a dog?"

Even on his death bed King Charles II was not without his beloved dogs; his Lord in Waiting recorded that he lay awake listening to the "Scotch Coal Fire" and that a dozen dogs came to his bed.

However the Royals' interest was not diminished when Charles's brother, James II, came to the throne, for he was another great dog lover. He obviously had his priorities right, for when sailing off the Scottish coast he was forced to abandon his ship. He gave the order "Save the dogs" but, luckily, he remembered he also had Colonel Churchill on board and, after a pause, added his name to the command!

The family name of Churchill is a famous one and associated with Blenheim Palace, in England, where the great English politician Winston Churchill was born. The Colonel Churchill sailing with James II became the Duke of Marlborough and he too formed a liking for the red and white spaniels, which took the name of Blenheim, or Marlborough Spaniels. It was while the Duke of Marlborough was away abroad, fighting the battle of Blenheim, that the legendary story was born about the blenheim spaniels which are the direct predecessors of the modern day Cavalier King Charles Spaniel.

It relates how Sarah, Duchess of Marlborough, was nursing an in-whelp spaniel in her lap

The Duke and Duchess of Marlborough with their children and Spaniels at Blenheim Palace.

Queen Victoria riding out, by Sir Francis Grant (1803-1878). The Royal Collection.

and, in her agitation awaiting news of her husband, repeatedly pressed her thumb on top of the bitch's head to comfort herself. When the great news arrived that the Battle of Blenheim had been won, the spaniel bitch had her litter of puppies all bearing the 'thumb print' on top of their heads, and the mark became known as the 'Blenheim spot'. Many years later this unique marking still appears on large numbers of blenheim Cavalier King Charles Spaniels.

The Royals' devotion to their pet spaniels was certainly reciprocated by their dogs – there is no better example of their devotion and loyalty to their owners than that of the black and white spaniel belonging to the ill-fated Mary Queen of Scots, who was executed in 1587. Documentation, too gruesome to quote, reveals how her dog refused to be left behind, accompanied her mistress to the execution, and remained hiding in the Queen's petticoats as she lay beheaded. Much kinder hands than her poor mistress had met took the little dog away and cleaned her up.

Queen Victoria became the next Royal to fall for the attractions of these charming little dogs. Her most famous dog was 'Dash'. Even on the day of her Coronation, she couldn't bear to be away from this pet for long. In that year of 1838 Sidney Lee wrote: "On returning to the Palace she hastily doffed her splendours in order to give her pet spaniel Dash its afternoon bath." The Royal connection has continued into present times. Our reigning Queen's sister, Princess Margaret, had a Cavalier called Rowley, who was frequently photographed with his owner.

Not only Royalty but world leaders and film stars too have discovered that having the Cavalier King Charles Spaniel as a pet is the ideal antidote to the stresses and strains brought upon them by their exacting and tedious public roles. In America President Reagan and his wife Nancy were often photographed with their attractive blenheim Cavalier, when the famous couple occupied the White House. The legendary crooner Frank Sinatra is known to be a breeder of the dogs.

In England a few years ago during the present Prime Minister's election campaign, the media were waiting patiently in the street outside the London town house of one of the candidates, Michael Heseltine. The television cameras quickly whirled into action as the front door opened, hoping for an exclusive shot, but instead out stepped one of Mr. Heseltine's daughters about to take the family's Cavaliers for their morning constitutional! Even the 'Iron Lady' of English politics, Margaret Thatcher, was captured on television being 'towed' along a beach by an enthusiastic tricolour Cavalier.

THE CAVALIER COLOURS

One of the greatest attractions of the Cavalier King Charles Spaniel is that they are available in four choices of colours to suit all tastes. The most common colour and the one most easy to breed is the blenheim. It is a rich chestnut colour, ideally well broken up on a pearly white background, and when freshly bathed the white areas have an exquisite sparkling glint. The blenheim's head should have a symmetrical white blaze so as to leave room for the much prized lozenge or 'Blenheim Spot' in the centre of the skull.

The tricolours should ideally be a glossy, raven black, again well broken up on a pearly white background. The French word 'tricolour' refers to the third colour on the variety, which should be a rich mahogany tan, and the tricolour Cavalier should be marked with this

Former American President Ronald Regan pictured with his wife, Nancy, and their Cavalier.

tan above the eyes and below the black eye-patches on the face. The tan should be found on the underside of the ear leathers, behind the elbows if the black markings extend that far, and under the tail. Dog show spectators will always see the judge examining the tricolour Cavaliers more closely than the other colours to see if the tan is present in the right places. The tan markings are likely to be missing on the dog if the black patches do not extend in the right places, as the tan can only be an extension of the black colour. 'Lemon' or yellowy washed-out tan is highly undesirable. Therefore it can be deduced that a first-class show tricolour is quite difficult to come by. The blenheims and tricolours are referred to as particolours.

The whole colours are the black and tans and rubies. The black and tan Cavalier should have a raven black coat with bright, rich tan markings above the eyes and on the cheeks of the head. The tan should be found on the underside of the ear leathers, on the chest and legs and on the underside of the tail. The rubies are one solid colour and that is the deepest rich red. The whole colours should carry no white patches. The choice of colours should be the

Ch. Salador Cegovia: The large, dark, lustrous eyes of the Cavalier contribute to the gentle, appealing expression. Photo: T. Morgan.

only difference in the Cavalier King Charles Spaniel when it comes to evaluating the whole dog as regards breed type, correct head pattern, make and shape and ideal size.

For a long time in the early beginnings and development of the breed, the quality and looks of the whole colours generally fell short of the particolours, although there were a few lovely individuals. But generally the whole colours were often referred to as the 'poor relations' and lived a Cinderella type of existence. However, this book reveals how certain breeders took up their case and, over the years, brought about a complete reversal in the wholecolour's fortunes.

THE BREED'S OUTSTANDING FEATURE

Probably the most outstanding feature of the breed and what initially first attracted me to it is the eyes, and indeed, as the pundits say, "The eyes have it."

One would be hard pressed to find another breed of dog with so gentle and appealing an expression as the Cavalier King Charles Spaniel. The eyes should be lustrous, large, dark and round without being prominent. A Cavalier with such eyes, found well-spaced in a well-balanced and beautifully marked head and complete with jet black nostrils and correct scissor bite, is likely to go a long way in the show ring, even if there are a few short-comings behind the collar.

LOOKING AT CAVALIERS

If someone is contemplating acquiring a Cavalier King Charles Spaniel, then the ideal way of seeing first-class specimens in all the four colours is to attend a general Championship show on Toy day or, better still, a Cavalier Club championship show organised by one of the different regional organisations. There the prospective owner can see puppy and adult dogs and talk to the different breeders and owners. A class full of top flight Cavaliers circling the ring is a great sight, and well-schooled show dogs really know how to display their virtues such as their lovely aristocratic heads proudly held on arched necks. The breed present a truly glamorous picture with their attractive colours, free-moving gait and wagging tails.

In Britain the general method of exhibiting Cavaliers is by standing and moving the individual exhibit on a loose lead, holding the dog's attention by hidden tidbits in the handler's pocket. The breed's gay and fearless temperament is shown to advantage with this method, and the Cavalier's active and glamorous appearance always draws a packed ringside. The competition is very keen indeed, as out of the hundreds of Cavaliers shown on the circuit each year, only an average of eight to ten dogs win their Championship titles.

GOOD BREEDING

Good specimens can be very difficult to breed with so many factors to consider at once. One has to look not only for a lovely head with all the glamour points, but correct conformation, a well-balanced body, and good movement. Breed type, quality and pleasing coats combining good markings and colouring are essential, plus the right temperament and show attitude. All this in the same dog! Another important factor is that the Cavalier bitch is not usually a prolific producer – singletons to just four or five in a litter is quite commonplace, and this, coupled with the range of four colours that it is possible to achieve in one litter, makes the choice of first-class specimens very limited.

On the other hand, Cavalier bitches make wonderful mothers and willingly nurse their puppies much longer than most breeds, spending a great deal of time playing with their young even after weaning. This devotion is often to the bitch's detriment when she gives everything to her puppies, and the breeder must, therefore, be very vigilant about Eclampsia or 'milk fever' developing. Fortunately with certain dietary additives and close supervision this problem can be avoided.

All these factors, coupled with the tough competition met at dog shows, makes the breeding and raising of high-class Cavaliers a daunting challenge. Many people do in fact come into the breed – and go out again almost at once! So much can go wrong up to show age that many 'promising show prospects' end up as much-loved pets in private homes. But of course many Cavalier owners would never dream of having their beloved pets criticised at dog shows and prefer to enjoy them just as they are as a breed – faithful and loving companion dogs.

THE ETHICS OF THE BREED

In Britain, right from the beginning, professionalism has been frowned upon and discouraged among the Cavalier breeders and owners, and particularly the handlers. Indeed today most breeders and owners still prefer to operate on an amateur hobby-style basis, although there are commercial kennels.

Discerning present-day breeders, who are still aware of the deep debt of gratitude that they owe to the pioneers of the breed, have tried to honour, and keep alive, their concepts. By discouraging professionalism they hoped to avoid anything unnatural and cosmetic, including keeping the breed 'free from trimming and artificial colouring'. Any amount of super-streamlined kennel blocks and complexes have never guaranteed the breeding of fabulous dogs, and indeed some of the greatest Cavaliers have been bred and raised in the most modest of surroundings and domestic confines.

By now, it is evident that the Cavalier King Charles Spaniel is a very special breed of dog. To have been owned by Royalty, world leaders and the very rich, those people who one would think have everything already, gives an insight into the appeal of the breed and why their owners readily find a place in their hearts and amongst their possessions for this breed of dog.

The Cavalier has an indefinable something in its make-up and character which enables it to lift the heart of its owner in the darkest of moments. It has been shown how, in highly charged situations, they are devoted and steadfast to their owners. Adaptable, undemanding and tolerant to their sometimes eccentric keepers, they possess an insatiable eagerness to join in with any activity, be it a stroll across Newmarket downs with their Royal master or a trip on the high seas.

If you are looking for an alert guard dog with follow-through, a super-slick gundog or an obedience work subject, then don't expect too much of the Cavalier or you can become disappointed. Although the Cavalier has unbounding enthusiasm for everything, there are, honestly, more suitable breeds of dogs for these pursuits.

The Cavalier King Charles Spaniel is essentially a devoted companion dog and 'Comforter' as depicted by their ancient ancestors, the Royal Toy spaniels in those old Masters' paintings. In this role the Cavalier King Charles Spaniel has few peers.

Chapter Two

PICKING PUPPIES

After making their selection of a suitable sire for their brood bitch, the breeder then eagerly awaits the arrival of the hopefully resultant litter with much anticipation. Nobody ever really gets exactly what they planned on breeding, but usually there is a puppy in the litter which eventually compensates for any disappointment there may be.

'LUCKY' MARKINGS

All the different breeders have their own individual techniques for picking puppies, and they develop an eye and knowledge of what the puppies should display at different ages. All bloodlines can be slightly different in appearance at an early age. Some breeders rely on a good knowledge of conformation and an eye for balance in a puppy, while others, even if they possess these talents, will still hold much store by the lucky markings and omens connected with dog breeding before examining the dog much more closely.

The great breeder Amice Pitt sometimes used to refer to the lucky 'Champion's elbow' marking seen on particolour dogs, where the blenheim or tricolour wholecolour is extended well over the elbow joints on both sides into the white forelegs. This lucky marking is well illustrated by Ch. Salador Crystal Gayle and Ch. Homerbrent Samantha, for instance.

Then there are the lucky 'Spots', the best known and most highly-prized one being the lozenge or thumb-print marking on the top of the head of blenheim Cavalier King Charles Spaniels. When two equally good blenheims are being appraised by the judge in a close decision, if one has the spot and the other does not, then this highly desirable marking will weigh heavily in the final decision and most likely in the direction of the lucky spot wearer.

One small dark spot on the bridge of the nose and close to the nostril of the tricolour Cavalier is also usually the sign of a lucky dog, whilst the same applies to the dog who has a small pale pigmented spot midway on the inside of the bottom lip.

In whole colours, where the dark colour extends over the whole of the foreleg and front foot, a small white spot of hair hidden on the underside of the pasterns, close to the upturned front pads, is considered by some to be very lucky indeed.

OMENS

Besides the lucky markings, some breeders rely on their inborn intuition and place a lot of store on any lucky omens they may receive. For instance, the mother of the puppies is not

A promising young puppy, with the lucky thumb-print on the head.

Ch. Salador Crystal Gayle showing the 'Champion's elbow' marking.
Photo: Diane Pearce.

always a bad judge of her own litter, and the puppy that the bitch frequently seems to keep and nurse between her front paws and under her chin is the one to watch out for.

The most memorable omen that I ever experienced was the day a spider picked out Ch. Salador Crystabelle when she was a few days old. From most newly-born litters I am usually able to pick out the best and most favourable-looking puppies quite quickly, but this day I was having great difficulty in separating a lovely and level litter of four blenheim puppies from Ch. Salador Crystal Gayle, sired by Ch. Homerbrent Samson.

Crouched in front of the whelping box while studying the litter, I suddenly became aware of a very large spider scurrying across the kitchen floor towards us. In amazement I watched it scramble over the side of the whelping box in a most purposeful way, and I was transfixed to see it climb on top of one puppy. After briefly waving a feeler over the puppy's head, the

Selected by a spider: Ch. Salador Crystabelle (second from left) at six weeks.

spider turned and left the box as quickly as it had come. After that extraordinary experience the puppy was well and truly earmarked – and grew up to become Ch. Salador Crystabelle!

THE SCIENTIFIC APPROACH

But an individual breeder naturally cannot keep relying on lucky markings and omens to pick out their best dogs, and sooner or later they must learn more about the science of their chosen subject.

When it comes down to learning the real thing, of course the markings of the dog have to be taken into consideration, but the breeder/owner, if intending to take up showing and breeding seriously, must sooner or later have to learn about correct conformation and acquiring an 'eye' for a dog in general. Of course many people are born with this gift and have a natural eye for picking out dogs and puppies without actually examining them too closely.

But the inexperienced person just starting out can learn much from the practical and physical laying on of hands taught to them by an experienced dog person. Such a person does not necessarily have to be another Cavalier King Charles Spaniel breeder, because the

Ch. Homerbrent Carnival at ten weeks.

A Millstone litter, bred by Evelyn Booth.

conformation of the Cavalier is much the same as many other breeds as regards the basic construction. In fact, it is almost better to be taught from an experienced and well-informed owner of a different breed who will give valuable and unbiased instruction to a keen novice willing to learn. The laying-on of hands and having a well-informed teacher present is far better than trying to learn one's craft from the pages of a book.

When choosing potential show puppies it is easier to pick an individual from a good-sized litter where there are a number of puppies to choose from, and you can compare one against another. The whole litter should ideally have been well-reared and be a level lot as regards size and body condition. This type of litter is to be favoured instead of a litter with only one good-looking individual amongst a group of poor-looking litter mates. A level litter with more than one very attractive puppy means that the litter was the result of a good breeding plan, and it is likely, after close examination and comparisonof the puppies, that there will be at least one top-class individual emerging as 'Promising' above the others.

The best time to examine the individual litter is when the puppies are eight to nine weeks old, and the event is rather like making up your own personal miniature dog show, and 'judging and placing' the puppies on individual merit.

EXAMINING CONFORMATION

Each puppy must be stood on a non-slip surface up on a table for an individual examination of all the conformation points, coat markings, teeth placement and temperament. Most of everything that is required in an adult dog is all there in miniature, even if one does have to look a bit closer. For instance, upright shoulders, short necks and long lower joints to the hind legs below the hocks will still be there when the dog eventually becomes an adult. Good conformation does not magically come as the dog grows up and matures; it is there from an early age.

Also at this age of eight to nine weeks, when the puppies become more impressionable, it is a good time to get them used to standing well on a table. This is achieved by holding each end of the puppy between front and hind legs with both hands and gently applying a rocking movement between the hands, slightly above the level of the table, where eventually, after several seconds, the puppy will be positioned correctly, standing foursquare; the forelegs being placed down correctly first, followed quickly by the hind legs set slightly more widely apart. The puppy's head and chin are supported securely by the left hand while the right hand makes the assessment, whilst at the same time the word 'Stand' is repeated, firmly but quietly, several times. If the puppy struggles, engage the original holding position and repeat the exercise.

It is always best to finish on a good note, so even if the puppy only stays still for a few seconds but does achieve a 'stand', the puppy must be given a lot of praise, hugs and kisses!

CHECKING TEETH FORMATION

One has to hazard a guess how the teeth formation will end up, but personally I like to see a scissor bite from the start in my own lines. A slightly undershot or level bite very occasionally crops up, recessive genes being what they are, even though I do not like using bad-mouthed stock in my breeding programme, but with the second teeth the mouth usually rights itself and ends up in a perfect bite. In some bloodlines I appreciate that the mouths can start wrong and then, with time, can finish perfectly all right, and vice versa!

Again eight to nine weeks is a perfect age to teach the puppy to show its teeth for examination; and it is a good time, well away from four to five months of age when the puppy starts changing its first teeth. At this stage the puppy will be extremely sore in the mouth and it is best to refrain from any forceful handling.

For teeth examination the puppy should preferably be held comfortably in the arms of an assistant, while the examiner gently draws the lips back to reveal the teeth for assessment. At the same time the examiner should repeat the word 'Teeth' several times firmly but quietly, and if a good response is achieved, the puppy should be given much praise and love.

On another day, and not too frequently, this teeth examination should then progress to the assistant steadying the puppy in a 'Sit' position on the non-slip table whilst the examiner makes the same check. The puppy learns to do away wih the security of being held close to the body and gradually learns to offer itself up for the table check. Gradually the 'Stand' and 'Teeth' lessons become combined and continued, but only until the puppy becomes confident and thoroughly used to this routine event. Too much training is as bad as too little training. This very valuable tuition will stand the puppy in good stead for the rest of its life as regards visits to the vet, day-to-day routine grooming and for exhibiting at dog shows. All lessons must be done with kindness and firmness, the commands given in a quiet voice with much praise and affection when good things are achieved.

ASSESSING THE MARKINGS

One of the surest things that can be safely assessed on the individual puppy is the colour and markings, even if the creature is a small one to look at.

The well-broken markings on the blenheims and tricolours are quite discernible from an early age, especially the tricolours. The blenheims may start off rather pale and powder-puff in appearance but, by turning the hair back, one can get a fair idea about where the blenheim markings extend to. The prized lozenge is always very noticeable. Ascertaining the depth of colour to which the adult blenheim Cavalier will mature is done by studying the depth of blenheim red around the eye rims and the underside of the ear flaps.

With a tricolour the black and white patches should ideally be well spaced and broken up, because with maturity the solid black tends to creep over the white areas and, with the coming of the longer adult coat, some white patches tend almost to disappear. The tan markings should be rich mahogany even at eight to nine weeks of age, and it is unlikely that lemon-shaded and washed out tan is likely to deepen much in colour. On a tricolour the most important check is to make sure that the puppy has the black markings extending well to and around the tail root, which provides the extension for the essential tan markings under the tail. Most top breeders do not like the black markings to go much lower than the rear hock joint, and certainly one black hind leg is very off-putting when viewing the eventual show adult moving away from one.

The wholecolour puppies should be marked as described in the Breed Standard but allowances can be made for several things at an early age which have a good chance of righting themselves by adulthood.

The black and tan puppies can start off with a slightly less depth of tan colour than is

Int. Ch. Sunninghill Perseus of Lochfee (left) pictured as a puppy.

desired in the adult Cavalier; the tan markings can also be rather sooty in appearance. If the sootiness clears by adulthood it usually means the individual is likely to end up with very rich tan. The ruby puppies can also start paler than the finished article turns out. The same check can be made as in the blenheim puppy, by judging the depth of colour around the eye rims and the underside of the ear flaps. But, of course, much credit should go to the puppy born with rich coat pigment in all the four colours.

A few white hairs may be present on young wholecolour puppies, chiefly seen on the forehead, chin, throat or chest or on the toes of the feet. When the puppy grows its adult coat, not only does the colour intensify but also the white hairs can become drowned out by the wholecolour creeping over them. But where there are very large patches of white on wholecolour puppies, the coming of the adult coat is not likely to make much difference to the individual's appearance, and the adult is termed 'Mismarked'.

THE IDEAL PUPPY

Viewing the puppy overall when standing on the table, the ideal promising puppy at eight to nine weeks should project a well-balanced look. As described in the explanation of the Breed Standard, there is a practical check one can make if one cannot judge 'balance' with the eye: it is that the length of the puppy's back from the peak of the withers to the tail root should be the same measurement as that from the withers to the bottom of the front pad resting on the table. The puppy should be unexaggerated in every other aspect of itself.

The leg bone should be moderate and in keeping with the size of the individual puppy, neither being too overdone nor too light in appearance. Big joints and feet usually mean big adults, whilst fine, spindly legs are equally undesirable and are not likely to improve even with excellent feeding.

The natural tail carriage of the individual puppy can be fairly assessed at an early age, and I would be very wary of keeping one back who carries its tail right over the back when moving around in a trot. It is a widely held belief that the true tail carriage can be assessed at mealtimes, when the puppies are all feeding around the dish. The ones who keep their tails well over the backs and straight up in the air are most likely to be the ones who mature into 'gay'-tailed adults. The tail should be held right down when feeding.

After studying the puppies closely, one by one, the breeder should have gained some idea of which are the best of the litter. They should, with time and experience, be able to cultivate an inner confidence when assessing puppies and learn to believe in and accept what they see, without other people's opinions.

The puppies the breeder has singled out from the rest of the litter must be particularly watched when they are turned loose in a large enough run. Much credit should be given to the eye-catching puppy who has stood up to a close examination and who now demonstrates its good conformation by moving around the run with a well-balanced and sound gait. One can make allowances for slightly loose elbows and gangly back legs, but the movement should be there, and the head and the tail held out nicely.

DIFFICULT ASSESSMENT AREAS

The two 'grey areas' in assessing young puppies are the heads and the temperament. As far as temperament is concerned, one must always be very firm but gentle when handling puppies and credit must be given to the puppy who is fairly bold when encouraged to come up for handling. A slight shyness is excusable until the puppies get used to a lot of handling and one can also meet with the very mischievous puppy who refuses to be caught and always seems to just dodge out of the reach of one's hand. Also one should not always 'write off' the shy puppy who dives back into the bed when a human being approaches, and a special effort must be made to pick that puppy up and give nursing and reassurance for several minutes every day. That way confidence will soon come to the puppy.

Years ago, when I bred Labrador Retrievers, I had such a puppy in a litter that always used to dive into the kennel as soon as she saw somebody coming, and stay hidden! I have now come to recognise this trait as that belonging to a puppy who is very sensitive, because that Labrador bitch puppy eventually went to be trained as a guide dog at Leamington Spa – and she qualified in half the time it normally takes to train a dog for this highly demanding role!

However, when a litter of puppies is having its 'mad half hour' and a good rough and tumble, I would be very suspicious of the individual who continually lays into its litter mates and pins them down on the floor in a really aggressive manner. With young show dogs one is never really sure of how they are going to behave when they finally get to be exhibited, but the early impressions usually run true to form. Only with a bitch puppy can one make allowances, for before a season she can behave quite out of character and be a little jumpy and nervous due to hormonal changes. If these hormonal imbalances do not right themselves, the young bitch may not be able to revert back to her cheerful, outgoing puppy character, and this change usually occurs around twelve months of age.

The head of the young puppy is the most difficult to assess, but there are certain positive features to look for.

At eight to nine weeks of age the eyes should be nicely rounded, dark and large for the size of the overall head. The ear leathers, when pulled down flat against the side of the head should reach the tip of the nose, even if the ear does have little or no ear fringes at that time. The stop should be shallow and the puppies that are born with a good bump on top of the bridge of the nose should now be displaying a nice, but not too long or too short a muzzle. In my own line the cushioning or 'choochiness' under the eyes is already there.

The nose pigment should be black, and when the puppy is taken outside in strong sunlight there should be no brown or pink hue to it. Much credit should be given to the puppy whose nose is already negroid in blackness. Personally I do not dislike small flesh marks, that is to say the small pink patches on the puppy's otherwise black nose, because it usually signifies very black adult pigment and, as the old breeders used to say, 'slow to come, slow to go'.

Flesh marks can sometimes take up to two years to fill in, but it is doubtful whether large areas will disappear. One of my brood bitches from years ago had a black piece come in her nose when she was four years old. Indeed, the event of a bitch having a litter certainly improves this condition. Nose pigment is a very important consideration when choosing puppies for future exhibition and breeding purposes and, all things being equal, a potentially excellent male becomes much more in demand for stud purposes when he possesses a coal black nose, and quite the reverse if his nose pigment is faulty.

Overall, the young puppy's head should give some impression as to how it is going to end up, and it is naturally enhanced by good markings and a nice blaze, as in the particolours. Breeders as a rule look for clear white markings on the muzzle. The unwanted freckles that usually start appearing from six to seven weeks onwards, plus the smudges that are there at birth, are sometimes enough for them to place the potential show puppy in a pet home, although one or two add a little 'character' to the face, not forgetting the lucky spot on the bridge of the tricolour's nose. Equally unwelcome is the 'roaning' or spots which appear in the white patches and on the legs of particolours. This can happen when the individual dog has whole colours close up in the pedigree.

Personally I do eventually give all my puppies and young adults this close examination of all the desired points, but not before I have stood well back and looked for a certain expression in the head; indeed, it sounds awful, but it is nearly always the feature the puppy or young dog is picked for before making any other close examination of its conformation and movement. What I look for is the impression and expression portrayed by the lower forehead and the eyes of the individual dog. When running around, it is the way the puppy suddenly halts and presents itself in an alert stance, its outloook, the look of sheer class. In horse racing circles it is called the 'look of eagles', and it is the keen, distant look of an animal with a far-reaching destiny. The rare individuals that possess this feature are usually, after further examination, pretty good behind the collar as well.

The 'look of eagles' is not always easy to capture in a photograph, but in this book the look is beautifully illustrated by photographs of Cavalier King Charles Spaniels such as Ch. Little Dorritt of Ttiweh, and Ch. Homerbrent Samantha. When choosing puppies and young dogs, it is the 'look' which singles them out from hundreds of others.

Chapter Three

CARING FOR YOUR CAVALIER

There is nothing quite like the joy of bringing a new puppy home to join the family circle and naturally the family will be anxious to do their best for the new arrival. This chapter suggests some guidelines to ensure that everything runs smoothly.

THE TECHNICAL SIDE

To avoid any heartache and bad feeling later, the most important step, before purchasing a new puppy, is to give the matter serious thought.

Prospective buyers are strongly recommended to see the new puppy with its litter mates and mother in the home where the puppy was bred. By buying from a private breeder, the new owner will almost surely receive an 'after-sales service' when worrying questions arise and, when the new owner goes on holiday, most breeders will consider taking the puppy back for boarding.

A conscientious breeder will always discuss with the prospective owner various points. These include the suitability of the sex of the puppy if the new owner already owns a dog, whether they are at home for periods of time during the day to care for the new puppy and whether they have a suitable home and secure back yard or garden.

Before purchasing a new puppy, although it is difficult to remember in all the excitement, the new owner must make quite clear to the breeder their intentions regarding the puppy. If the new owner only wants a pet dog, then the breeder will take them at their word. The new owner may only be offered a 'pet' quality puppy and the breeder is likely to place restrictions on the puppy's Kennel Club papers – for instance, to say that the puppy cannot enter dog shows or that its progeny cannot be registered by the Kennel Club. Endorsements can be lifted by the breeder at a later date but, to save any bad feeling or misunderstanding at the time of purchase, the new owner must make their intentions clear. If necessary something may have to be put in writing.

A new owner is perfectly entitled to ask for a veterinary certificate to ensure that they are buying a puppy free from disease and any inherited abnormalities. But most discerning breeders usually give a verbal assurance that, should the new puppy fail to satisfy a veterinary check after leaving the breeder, or becomes unwanted for any other reason, the purchaser can take the puppy back to its original home. The veterinary check should then be made within a short space of time after the purchase of the puppy. Remember, most discerning breeders sell their puppies with all good intentions and that nobody can put a guarantee on a live animal indefinitely.

That is why it is so important to purchase the puppy from a private breeder who is, hopefully, emotionally involved, rather than buying a second-hand animal from a dealer who has no personal involvement.

ARRIVING HOME

If the family already own different pets, then it is very important that the new puppy be properly introduced to them from the safety of the owner's arms and under close supervision. If the puppy ever has to be left alone in a room where other pets are present then a play-pen, or a travelling crate or cage, is an invaluable item of equipment. Besides safeguarding the puppy, this type of equipment is excellent for ensuring that 'accidents' do not happen on the best carpets. The puppy will expect to be taken out at regular intervals to relieve itself in the back garden. Here another play-pen can be erected on the lawn, or patio, or in an area where the owner wants the puppy to perform its duty. In time the puppy will learn to be clean in the house and will usually whimper and ask to go out when feeling uncomfortable. If the puppy is running loose in the house, the normal indication that something is about to happen is when the puppy runs around in tight circles, tail up! Always place the puppy outside after waking or eating and at suitable intervals during the day.

FOLLOWING THE BREEDER'S INSTRUCTIONS

All conscientious breeders provide a diet sheet and a record of worming dates plus any immunisation treatment the puppy may have already received. Follow the breeder's instructions to the letter as regards the amounts and ingredients of the diet. The puppy has been used to that food and any change may cause unwanted diarrhoea which may be difficult to cure. In time the new owner may wish to continue with, or to change, the type of food being fed to the puppy so as to fit in with their own theories on raising a puppy and their own individual life style. This needs to be done with care.

It is a good idea to take the puppy to meet the family's veterinary surgeon shortly after arrival, first of all to have the puppy checked over to confirm that the new acquisition is a healthy one, and also to discuss and arrange an immunisation programme. The vet will be pleased to discuss the puppy's feeding regime as well.

The new puppy can be protected from all known canine diseases either by injected vaccines or by a combined homoeopathic nosode. The choice rests entirely with the owner. Until this process has been completed it is very unwise to take the puppy into public places frequented by other dogs, or to allow friends to bring their own dogs into the new puppy's home. Their dogs may look perfectly all right but they can still be the carrier of a canine disease.

MANAGING THE NEW PUPPY

Besides the first stages of house training and regular mealtimes, the new puppy must be allowed to rest and have regular sleep periods. For this purpose a comfortable bed must be provided, with suitable bedding that can be removed for laundering, in a draught-free place

Ready to go... Ch. Salador Connors safely stowed away in his travelling cage for a comfortable journey. The metal travelling cage has a removable padded floor. It is light and airy, with plenty of vision all-round. The plastic travelling box (right) has ventilation slits and one opening end. This is more suitable for cold journeys, and it is the only type accepted for air flights.

and with no overhead noises. This is the puppy's own area, a place the puppy will come to rely on for peace and quiet, which must be respected by the owner if they want a sane, well-adjusted companion dog. From the first night the puppy spends in its new home, the owner must start as they mean to go on. It is very unfair to let the puppy spend a night in the warm, cosy bed of its owner and then expect the puppy to keep quiet when left alone downstairs the next night in a cold, dark kitchen. An easy compromise is to allow the puppy to sleep next to the owner's bed in a warm, secure travelling box. A cuddly toy, or a ticking clock placed under the puppy's blanket to mimic the mother's heart-beat, are well-tried comforters.

The enclosed run in the garden is an ideal place to put the puppy, for example first thing in the morning when all the family are bustling around the kitchen where the puppy may accidentally get stepped on.

A Cavalier King Charles Spaniel puppy is neither physically nor mentally up to going on long walks with the family and may have to be carried most of the way in the safety of the owner's arms. Serious exercising, and then only by moderate degrees, can take place when the puppy has finished growing, usually at around seven months of age.

Meanwhile in the home the owner can get the puppy used to wearing a light puppy collar and occasionally, when supervised, attach the lead on to the collar, which gets the puppy used to trotting around with a lead trailing behind. Skating along highly polished floors, climbing stairs and jumping on and off high furniture must not be allowed: it is not only dangerous but may affect the puppy's soft bones and conformation for later life.

LEAD TRAINING
The easiest way of training a puppy to walk on a lead is to go the way the puppy wants to go! To encourage the puppy to follow you, walk backwards tapping the ground or patting the knees. For verbal encouragement there was never a better word than the one used by the

famous dog trainer, Mrs Barbara Woodhouse – Walkies! Training sessions should be short and stress-free for the puppy. Always remember to finish on a good note with lots of praise. Try not to be tempted to keep picking the puppy up, or else the puppy will keep stopping in anticipation of a free ride.

If the owner already has a small, well-trained dog, then the ideal way is to let the puppy learn from the older dog by keeping the puppy on a lead between the owner and the steadier adult dog as the group walk along.

At four to five months it is better to cease lead training as the puppy will be teething and may be feeling very sore in the mouth. Also at this time the puppy may go off eating for the same reason. I always keep my own puppies rather on the bonny side from the weaning stage in case this happens, and then they have reserves to fall back on.

BASIC TRAINING
For safety purposes the indoor travelling box comes in as an invaluable item when the puppy's owner decides to go for a journey, particularly when driving a car alone. Otherwise the puppy is best held in the lap of one passenger in the car and will be less prone to car sickness that way.

When the puppy is old enough and big enough to stand up to serious training, say at eight to twelve months of age, some proper basic training will be invaluable for the rest of the dog's life.

All pet dogs should at least be taught the three commands Sit, Heel and Stay. The command Sit is invaluable, for example, when close supervision is required by the owner or the vet. The command Heel makes the walking of the dog a pleasurable experience, not a nightmare, and Stay has saved many a dog's life when the owner has used it in the nick of time to stop a dog from running across a road in front of oncoming traffic.

Besides the wonderful social aspects of the local dog training club, the new owner with their puppy will receive expert tuition and guidance for the future. Here is a chance to train your Cavalier to high standards of obedience and eventually to compete in organised competitions.

For the puppy destined hopefully for the show ring there are specialised training clubs known as Ring Craft classes. These can also be used, for the social aspect, by the owner who does not want their dog too regimented in behaviour. Dogs just love words beginning with T and the three most important words that a show dog can learn are Teeth, Trot and Treat. Teeth is self-explanatory – a show dog's teeth are examined scores of times. Trot is where the show dog must be under control at the handler's side but not robotic nor regimented like the obedience-trained dog. The last thing the handler wants is a show dog to Sit when the process of walking around the ring is finished! When the show handler approaches the judge after showing the dog in a free trotting gait, the dog must stand square, looking up at the handler with an alert expression and a wagging tail, on a loose lead. Given the signal Treat, the show dog soon becomes cute in understanding what this means and, as the judge turns away to appraise the next dog on the table the treat, usually a tasty piece of liver, is deposited in the waiting mouth!

GROOMING THE NEW PUPPY

Specialised advice is given in this chapter on grooming the show Cavalier puppy and adult, but the basic advice can easily apply to the pet Cavalier whose owner is anxious that the dog should look in pristine condition.

A young puppy must be introduced to, and gently handled in, regular grooming sessions, held in the arms for safety initially and then graduating on to a non-slip table surface. A soft-bristled brush is the main instrument used to groom the new puppy until the feathering grows in adulthood, when other grooming tools are required. Nails must be checked for overgrowth and the white tips neatly trimmed away, keeping well away from the pink quicks. The ears should be smelt and examined carefully for any ear infection and canker. Occasional baths leave the puppy's coat silky clean and free from vermin. Make sure the puppy is absolutely bone dry before placing outside.

DETAILED GROOMING

Grooming is not just about bathing and brushing the Cavalier King Charles Spaniel. The presentation of each dog is the result of the combination of certain factors which the dog has experienced on a regular basis and, if the dog has not enjoyed the best elements of dog-keeping, then no amount of bathing and grooming will compensate.

Grooming tools and equipment.
Top row, left to right: Flexi-lead for controlled exercising; martingale chain collar (14ins) for show or home, fitted with a nylon lead and strong clip; dual-action two-tiered comb (for removing dead undercoat and combing long feathering); pin-wire slicker brush (available in different sizes, including one for sensitive skin).
Bottom row left to right: Mason Pearson hair brush; guillotine nail-clippers; plier nail-clippers (for curled-under over-grown nails); tooth-scaler (with left and right hand combined). All displayed on a non-slip rubber-topped grooming table.

REGULAR CHECKS

Most Cavaliers naturally wear their nails down level with the bottom of the foot pad. When using the guillotine nail-clippers correctly, the straightest handle should be nearest to the operator. Take great care and only take off the curved tips, keeping well away from the pink quicks in white-nailed dogs. With black-nailed dogs, a safe estimate has to be made, but the quick is still discernible if the underside of the claw is studied carefully. Salador Cegovia is nicely relaxed, because she knows she is not going to get hurt by her mistress!

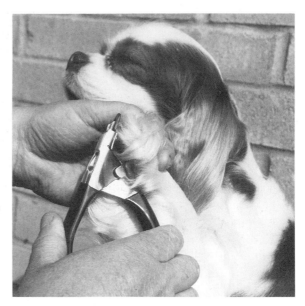

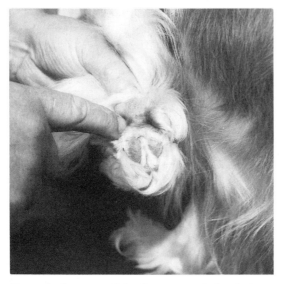

Turn the bottom of the feet up and check that there are no hard wedges of hair, tar or grit lodged between the pads. It is permissible and necessary on a show Cavalier to trim off the feathering on the underside of the foot, and between the underside of the toes. Check the general condition of the feet, and the creases between the toes, for any cuts or soreness.

Never touch the silky tassels of hair between the toes on top of the foot! They are part of the charm of the Cavalier King Charles Spaniel, and the owner may be heavily penalised by a show judge for trimming, which is forbidden in this breed.

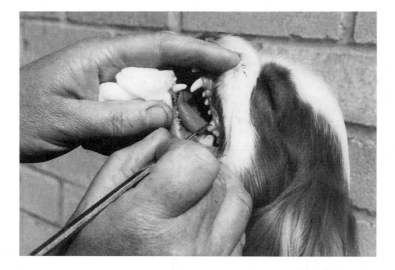

With a tooth-scaler, make regular checks of the teeth and gums, scraping away any brown tartar that builds up on the teeth. Scrape gently from the edge of the gum down the tooth. Finish by swabbing the teeth and gums with cotton-wool, soaked with a dental antiseptic fluid, obtainable from most pharmacists. Try not to let any residue drip into the dog's mouth, as this makes a bad taste. For gum disease, or loose or decaying teeth, seek veterinary advice. If the dog is a show specimen, the owner must discuss the treatment fully with the vet before any work is carried out. Extractions or extensive dental work must be backed up with a course of suitable antibiotics, as it is a widespread belief that neglecting to do this may lead to heart and kidney disease.

Use cotton-wool, soaked in an eye and stain-removing lotion, to gently wipe underneath the eye from the inside corner. Keep changing the cotton-wool for a dry piece and wiping, until the white hair is silky, clean and dry. Stains do not show on wholecolour Cavaliers, but the eye channel must still be kept clean and dry, and so this should be part of the regular grooming process.

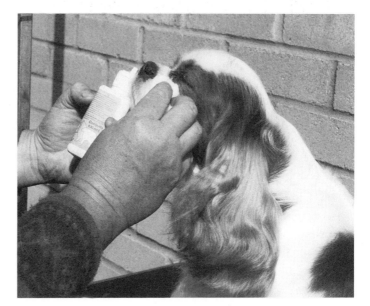

BATHING TIPS

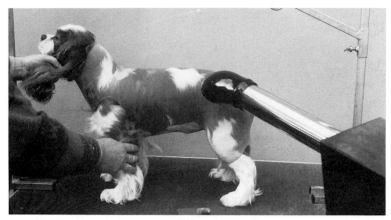

Regular bathing should keep your Cavalier's coat clean and healthy, but care must be taken when drying in order to keep the coat lying flat. An effective method is to power-dry through a stocking, which is made by opening the toe part on one leg section of a pair of tights. Two conveniently placed holes take the two front legs, while the rest is pulled over the whole of dog's body down to the hocks. This is useful for straightening and flattening thick, wavy-coated dogs. Slick the hair absolutely straight when it is wet, working with the lie of the hair, before fitting the stocking. Keep checking that the coat is lying flat, as the stocking is pulled down over the dog.

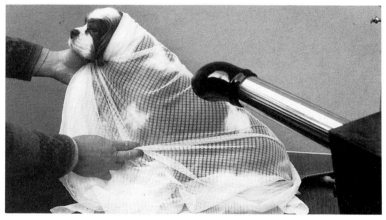

Use an old, clean net-curtain for a dog with a straighter, thinner and longer coat, to avoid that flattened look, and to produce a glamorous finish. Dry in sections, using the curtain as a protection for the straight, completed sections, and for blow-drying the wet areas. The power drier, fixed on a stand, leaves both hands free to steady the dog and to hold the curtain down firmly against the blast of warm air. The curtain also traps the warm air around the dog, which speeds up the drying process, thus avoiding the risk of a chill. It is also easier than constantly taking a stocking off, to check how the hair looks underneath.

GROOMING YOUR CAVALIER

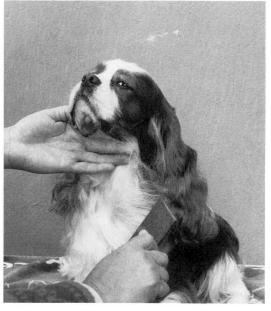

Using a slicker-brush, groom upwards, from well under the forelegs, with gentle, purposeful strokes.

Brush out the chest hair in layers, moving sideways left to right, using the free hand to hold the ungroomed hair out of the way.

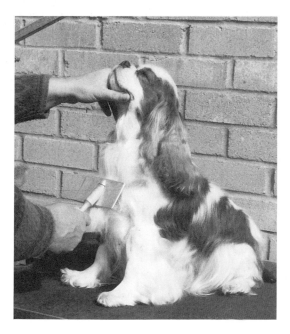

Complete by downward strokes until the slicker-brush glides effortlessly through the completed section, without feeling any snags on the brush.

The grooming 'arm' in use. The nylon neck strap holds the dog safely, while both hands are busy. Continue working from the chest over the whole of the dog's body, starting from the back of the head, using long, purposeful strokes. Empty the slicker-brush when it is full of hair. Run the comb through each section as it is finished, making sure that every hair is parted and free of knots.

Grooming is therapeutic for both dog and handler. This is an easy and relaxing way to complete the underarm, stomach and leg feathering, grooming as the dog lies stretched out on its side. Tease and pull apart any mats with the fingers, before using the slicker-brush. After ten years of regular grooming sessions, Ch. Salador Connors knows the routine all too well.

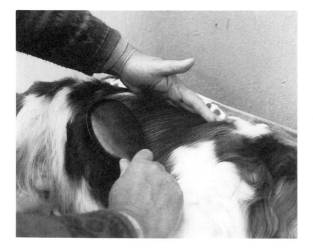

Using the bristle brush, complete the body grooming. Use the flat palm of the free hand alternately, in purposeful strokes going with the lie of the hair.

To groom the back legs safely, tether the dog with the nylon neck strap. Give support by passing the arm under the dog's body, and, holding the tail and the far hindleg firmly out of the way with one hand, groom carefully down the long feathering with the slicker-brush. After ensuring that no knots are present, draw the comb through to finish. Use the tail and the hand to protect the rear.

Work the opposite way round to groom the other hindleg. Complete by slicking and combing the tail feathering. It is easiest to do this by placing the dog in the Sit, and fanning the tail out over the grooming table. Another way to groom the tail is by turning it inwards and spreading it out along the dog's hip and lower body for support, as the long feathering is slicked out with long strokes.

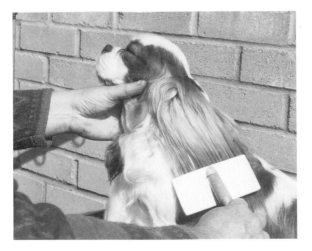

Groom the ears last of all, and take plenty of time over them. Turn the ear inside out, using the dog's neck and shoulder to support the flattened and spread out feathering. Groom and free the bottom couple of inches, until the slicker is gliding through without any snagging. Work back towards the ear base, with gentle downward strokes.

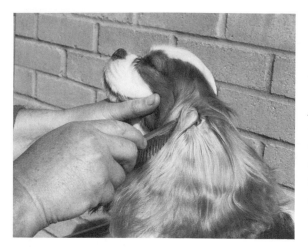

With the comb held in a vertical position, and, using the first few teeth only, start with gentle, probing, downward strokes from the side of the head into the corner of the ear. Free any lumps of hair carefully, by taking minute amounts of hair at one time. Finish with the slicker and, last of all, with the comb, held in a horizontal position.

Turn the ear over to the right side, and repeat the procedure, freeing the bottom couple of inches of the ear first with the slicker. Free any knots or wedges by teasing and pulling out with the fingers, before using any grooming tools. Take some time over this to avoid damaging and losing any valuable ear feathering. When you are satisfied that everything possible has been done with the fingers, use the grooming tools again.

With the held comb in a vertical position, start well back in the neck hair behind the base of the ear. Take gentle, purposeful strokes, using the first few teeth of the comb. Work, right to left, back towards the head, taking minute amounts of hair at a time, until any lumps are teased out and removed.

Finish by slicking the full length of the ear sideways. This is done by parting and taking up small sections of the ear feathering at one time, until the slicker glides through in one smooth movement. Comb through both ears, making sure the ear hair is absolutely free of knots and dead hair.
Before leaving the ears, check for any signs of canker or ear inflammation. Canker has a unmistakable, pungent smell, and it is usually accompanied by a heavy, waxy discharge. Neglect in treating ear canker, apart from the obvious medical implications, results in the dog rubbing and scratching most of the ear feathering away.

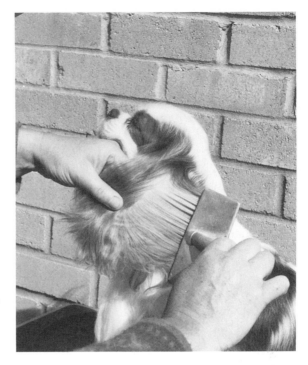

Good grooming and presentation are not sprayed on the outside; they come from healthy eating inside and being kept in a clean, healthy outdoor environment for most of the daylight hours. For instance, Cavaliers kept in centrally heated houses do not have the necessity to grow a full show coat and seem to be perpetually casting hair. Likewise kennel dogs confined to small urine-soaked concreted runs exhibit the telltale signs of their sad existence with their yellow stained legs. These conditions are hardly conducive to good coat presentation.

Ideally show dogs and well-kept pets should be accustomed to being exercised at regular times over clean grassland where the act of running through long, damp grass cleans the leggings and feet and is known to eventually remove yellow staining. Dogs can then return to their clean, dry sleeping and living accommodation which remains unfouled.

The individual house pet presents few problems for their owner but where breeders keep more than a few dogs, many prefer to keep their outdoor kennels and covered-run floors protected with a thin layer of clean, white pine shavings or coarse white sawdust. A mixture of both is ideal and the flour in the sawdust keeps the whites of the dog's coat sparkling, whilst the kennel floors remain dry and sweet smelling, even when accidents occur.

Grooming, with minimum damage to the coat and feathering, is made all that much easier by only brushing and combing an absolutely bone-dry and silky, clean coat. If the owner is anxious to avoid any damage to their furnishings and discomfort to their dog, then it is advisable not to groom dirty and sticky feathering. By the same token, the metal comb should be the last instrument the groomer uses to draw through the coat, and then only with a comb with the teeth gauge as illustrated. A flea comb with minute teeth spaces is a devastating instrument to use on a show dog with full bell-shaped ears. Better to deal with fleas through other methods.

Regular baths help to keep the Cavalier's coat clean and of the correct silky texture and many breeders have their own favourite shampoos and sprays. Personally I always use a regular insecticidal shampoo with a dash of dish-washing liquid in the dilution. This always produces the finish I like without using coat sprays. I prefer to spend my money on the best possible food for the dogs with a view to growing lovely show coats than on new-fangled shampoos and coat preparations.

Cavaliers enjoy sitting in a bath full of warm water being lathered up, but it is a mistake to give a final rinse to the dog with the same water. To ensure no soap residue and white flakes will be left on the skin and coat when dry, the final rise should be with clean, running water preferably using a shower-head spray. Empty plastic dish-washing liquid dispensers make ideal containers for mixing shampoos in and for squirting the mixture on to the desired areas. They are easy to grasp with wet hands, unbreakable and handy for floating in the bath water while lathering the dog up.

After the final rinse the dog should be wrapped up completely in a large fluffy bath towel, enclosing the ears in the folds of the towel, and left for a few minutes for the moisture to be absorbed. This removes the need to rub the coat and feathering too much. Then the dog is ready for a blow dry with a proper dog dryer to ensure a show finish.

The individual pet dog can be dried using an ordinary human hand-held hairdryer, but it takes a long time and the finish is not the same.

Your Cavalier is like a car – look after the motor and the exterior and it should hopefully last its owner a long time!

Chapter Four

THE BREED STANDARD

THE BRITISH BREED STANDARD

GENERAL APPEARANCE: Active, graceful and well-balanced with gentle expression.

CHARACTERISTICS: Sporting, affectionate, absolutely fearless.

TEMPERAMENT: Gay, friendly, non-aggressive, no tendency towards nervousness.

HEAD & SKULL: Skull almost flat between the ears. Stop shallow. Length from base of stop to tip of nose about one and a half inches. Nostrils black and well developed without flesh marks, muzzle well tapered. Lips well developed but not pendulous. Face well filled below eyes. Any tendency to snipiness undesirable.

EYES: Large, dark, round but not prominent; spaced well apart.

EARS: Long, sct high, with plenty of feather.

MOUTH: Jaws strong, with a perfect, regular and complete scissor bite, i.e. the upper teeth closely overlapping the lower teeth and set square to the jaws.

NECK: Moderate length, slightly arched.

FOREQUARTERS: Chest moderate, shoulders well laid back, straight legs moderately boned.

BODY: Short-coupled with good spring of rib. Level back.

HINDQUARTERS: Legs with moderate bone; well turned stifle – no tendency to cow or sickle hocks.

FEET: Compact, cushioned and well feathered.

Ch. Salador Celtic Maid (Ch. Salador Celtic Prince – Ch. Salador Coppergleam: Top Cavalier 1984, Toy Group winner – "A glorious mover."

Owned and bred by Sheila Smith.

The Cavalier skeleton (based on the photograph of Ch. Salador Celtic Maid).

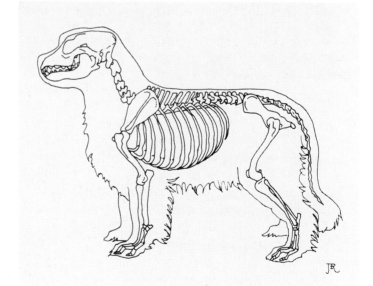

TAIL: Length of tail in balance with body, well set on, carried happily but never much above the level of the back. Docking optional. If docked, no more than one third to be removed.

GAIT: Free moving and elegant in action, plenty of drive from behind. Fore and hind legs move parallel when viewed from in front and behind.

The captivating head of Ch. Millstone Folly of Magjen.

Ch. Caroline of Homerbrent, owned by Molly Coaker, exemplifies the head and breed type synonymous with the prefix.

COAT: Long, silky, free from curl. Slight wave permissible. Plenty of feathering. Totally free from trimming.

COLOURS: Recognised colours are:
Black and Tan: Raven black with tan markings above the eyes, on cheeks, inside ears, on chest and legs and underside of tail. Tan should be bright. White marks undesirable.
Ruby: Whole coloured rich red. White markings undesirable.
Blenheim: Rich chestnut markings well broken up, on pearly white ground. Markings evenly divided on head, leaving room between ears for much-valued lozenge mark or spot (a unique characteristic of the breed).
Tricolour: Black and white well spaced, broken up, with tan markings over eyes, cheeks, inside legs, and on underside of tail.
Any other colour or combination of colours most undesirable.

WEIGHT AND SIZE: Weight – twelve to eighteen pounds. A small well-balanced dog well within these weights desirable.

FAULTS: Any departure from the foregoing points should be considered a fault and the seriousness with which the fault should be regarded should be in exact proportion to its degree.

Reproduced by kind permision of the English Kennel Club.

THE AMERICAN BREED STANDARD
Drawn up by The Cavalier King Charles Spaniel Club USA, Inc.

GENERAL APPEARANCE: An active, graceful, well-balanced dog, very gay and free in action; fearless and sporting in character, yet at the same time gentle and affectionate.

HEAD: The skull is slightly rounded, but without dome or peak; it should appear flat because of the high placement of the ears.

EYES: Large, round and set well apart; color a warm, very dark brown, giving a lustrous, limpid look. There should be slight cushioning under the eyes, which contributes much to the sweet, gentle expression characteristic of the breed. Faults: Small, almond-shaped, prominent or light eyes; white surrounding ring.

NOSE: There should be a shallow stop and the length from the base of the stop to tip of nose should be at least one and a half inches. Nostrils should be well developed and the pigment uniformly black. Putty or "dudley" noses and white patches on the nose are serious faults, as are small, pinched nostrils.

MUZZLE: Well tapered; mouth level; lips well covering. Faults: Sharp, pointed or snipey muzzle. Full or pendulous lips. Flesh marks, i.e. patches of pink pigment showing through hair on muzzle.

TEETH: Strong and even, preferably meeting in a scissors bite, although a level bite is permitted. Undershot mouths are greatly to be discouraged; it should be emphasized however that a slightly undershot bite in an otherwise well-balanced head with the correct, sweet expression should not be penalized in favor of a level mouth with a plain or hard expression. Faults: Weak or crooked teeth, crooked jaws.

EARS: Set high, but not close, on top of the head. Leather long with plenty of feathering and wide enough so that when the dog is alert, the ears fan slightly forward to frame the face.

NECK: Fairly long without throatiness, well enough muscled to form a slight arch at the crest. Set smoothly into nicely sloping shoulders.

SHOULDERS: Sloping back gently with moderate angulation to give the characteristic look of top class and elegance.

BODY: Short coupled with the ribs well sprung but not barrelled. Chest moderately deep, leaving ample heart room. Back level leading into strong, muscular hindquarters. Slightly less body at the flank than at the rib, but with no tucked-up appearance.

LEGS: Forelegs straight and well under the dog, bone moderate, elbows close to the sides. Hindlegs moderately muscled; stifles well-turned; hocks well let down. The hindlegs, viewed from the rear, should parallel each other from hock to heel. Pasterns strong and feet compact with well-cushioned pads. The dog stands level on all four feet. Faults: loose elbows; crooked legs; stifles turned in or out; cow hocks; stilted action; weak pasterns; open feet.

TAIL: Set so as to be carried level with the back. Tail should be in constant characteristic motion when the dog is in action.

DOCKING: Docking is optional, but whether or not the tail is docked, it must balance the body. If docked, tail must not be cut too short; two thirds is the absolute minimum to be left on the body, and the tails of broken-coloured dogs should always be docked to leave a white tip.

COAT: Long and silky and very soft to the touch; free from curl, though a slight wave is permissible. Feathering on ears, legs and tail should be long, and the feathering on the feet is a feature of the breed.

TRIMMING: No trimming of the dog is permitted. However it is permissible and often desirable to remove the hair growing between the pads on the underside of the foot.

SIZE: Height twelve to thirteen inches at the withers; weight proportionate to height, between thirteen and eighteen pounds. These are ideal heights and weights; slight variations are permissible, and a dog should be penalized only in comparison with one of equal appearance, type and quality. The weedy specimen is as much to be penalized as the oversized one.

COLORS: The following colors are the only colors acceptable:
1. Blenheim – Rich chestnut markings well broken up on a pearly white ground. The ears must be red and the color evenly spaced on the head, with a wide white blaze between the ears, in the centre of which is the much-valued lozenge (diamond) or 'Blenheim Spot'. The lozenge is a unique and highly desirable, though not essential, characteristic of the Blenheim.
2. Tricolor – Jet black markings well broken up on a pearly white ground, with rich tan markings over the eyes, on cheeks, inside ears and on underside of tail.
3. Ruby – Whole colored rich red.
4. Black and Tan – Jet black with rich tan markings over eyes, on cheeks, inside ears, on chest, legs and underside of tail.

FAULTS: White marks on whole-colored specimens, heavy ticking on Blenheims or Tricolors.

It is important to remember that a dog can have one or more of the faults listed in the Standard, in moderation, and still be an overall typical, gay, elegant Cavalier. On the other hand, bad temper or meanness are not to be tolerated and shall be considered to be disqualifying faults. It is the typical gay temperament, combined with true elegance and "royal" appearance which are of paramount importance in the breed.

Following recognition by the American Kennel Club in January 1995, the Breed Standard will be written and approved by the AKC. However, it is envisaged that any changes will be minor, with a few additions for descriptive purposes.

ANALYSIS OF THE STANDARDS

At their best the individual Cavalier King Charles Spaniel should present an overall picture of *glamour*. This effect is created largely by the excellence of the head pattern and length of ear leathers, but mostly by the dog's wealth and texture of coat, which include the richness and intensity of the colour. The blenheims and tricolours are assisted greatly by the characteristic and exquisite pearly glint in their white patches. Equally the black and tans and rubies can achieve a glamorous effect by the intensity and richness of colours when these qualities accompany the straightness and length of a highly glossed show coat. Because the whole colours are a little plainer in appearance than the particolours, it is important that the headpiece should be right. The whole colour Cavalier's head should be the exact pattern of the first class particolour Cavalier head, with all the little subtle differences, including the correct stop and tapered muzzle of correct length, generous, slightly rounded skull with correctly hung leathers of good length. The whole colour's eyes and nose pigment in particular have to be so correct and these important features are accentuated more in the plainer colour.

THE HEAD

On the old system the head of the Cavalier used to be scored on 50 out of 100 points, and it is still the most important feature of a true and typical Cavalier King Charles Spaniel. Over the years the true breed head, type, quality and characteristic temperament have come to be aligned with soundness and correct movement in a way that has never been known before.

I could write pages describing the subtle differences which combine to make up the first-class Cavalier head, without conveying satisfactorily to the reader what they are. However, the photographs in this book illustrate some of the best, and the reader can deduce from them what is ideally required to create the right impression. The main essentials are the quality of the eyes and the expression they impart, aided and abetted by the subtle features surrounding them, such as the correct stop, the cushioning under the eyes, the length of muzzle and the lip finish and nose pigment.

Some great Cavalier heads of the past were not necessarily perfect in some details but they were still able to impart that truly appealing and 'perfect' expression of a true Cavalier. In short, a Cavalier is not a Cavalier without a 'Head'; indeed the head on any pedigree dog is the first thing the eyes drop on, and gives an immediate impression of the type and quality of the animal before any detailed examination is undertaken.

Susan Burgess's blenheim stud dog, Ch. Crisdig Leading Seaman: Considered by many experts to have the perfect head.

Photo: Peter Dinmont.

Female perfection: The blenheim bitch Bredonvale Ttiweh L'Avengro.

Correct: Balanced head, with correct, bite, eyes and stop.

Incorrect:
Undershot bite.

Incorrect:
No stop, plain head.

Incorrect:
Stop too deep, domed
head, low-set ears.

Incorrect:
Snipey, eyes too small,
muzzle too long, no
cushioning under eyes.

Incorrect:
Houndy lips.

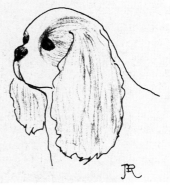

Incorrect:
Face too short,
stop too deep.

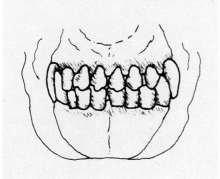

Correct:
Scissor bite.

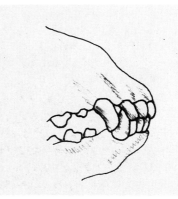

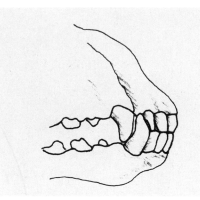

Level bite: No longer permitted in the UK.

NECK AND SHOULDERS

If someone were to ask me what would be the most important feature of a Cavalier or, for that matter any other breed of dog, then I would be strongly tempted to say 'the head', but I will refrain and go on to say it would be the neck and shoulders. In other breeds of dogs, especially working ones where body conformation, soundness, and precise, athletic movement is given greater priority and is more highly favoured than a great head, an owner can possibly get away with a dog with an otherwise plain head. But not in a top class Cavalier King Charles Spaniel!

A dog who is born with a really first class neck and shoulders is indeed blessed, and the feature stays with them life long. The correct neck and shoulder set has the happy knack of setting off everything in front of it and everything behind it. To determine whether a young dog, hopefully destined for the show ring, is in possession of such an important feature, a close examination of it must be made.

In the case of a small dog such as the Cavalier, the examination should be made on the non-slip surface of a table when the dog is standing relaxed and with all four legs correctly positioned and, in this description, with the head being to your left and the tail to the right.

The left hand determines a clean-throated dog with a good length of neck, the forechest feeling nicely convex in shape and sweeping gracefully well behind and slightly below the level of the elbows. With a closed fist it should be impossible to bury the hand in the chest cavity between the front legs. The forechest should fill the breadth of the extended palm and feel convex to the touch.

The FRONT LEGS should be straight and drop absolutely vertical when viewed from the front or side, through strong and straight pasterns, into cat-like feet, which are well-padded with the breed's characteristic tassels of hair displayed between the toes.

The LEG BONE should be of moderate quality and in keeping with the balance and size of the individual dog. The bone should be neither too heavy nor too fine in appearance.

The TOE NAILS in a dog which has adequate exercise and has access to all types of surfaces should display nails which are worn off naturally level with the bottom of the pad.

The DEWCLAWS, the fifth claw found on the inside of the ankle or pastern which can be present on all four legs, should ideally have been removed when the dog was a few days old.

Correct forequarters.

Incorrect:
Pigeon-toes or toeing in.

Incorrect:
Too narrow.

Incorrect:
Tied in at
elbow.

Incorrect:
Loose and
protruding
elbows, slack
in pasterns.

Many people argue that to remove the dewclaws is a mutilation of the dog, but if they had seen as many dogs over the years as I, as a professional groomer, have, which have been mutilated by their own dewclaws growing into their legs, the argument would stop right there. I remember one cross-bred terrier I was grooming for a customer was wearing his hind dewclaws like earrings! The claws had grown round in a circle through the flesh and out and around again in another circle. Besides the torture the dog has to endure, the consequences of having to deal with a dog with ingrowing dewclaws is quite obvious. Since the majority of most breeders' puppies end up in pet homes, the removal of the dewclaws is a simple little service they can do for their puppies to ensure that this never happens to them when they go out of their sight, and in case their new owners do not make a regular check on the claw growth.

In smooth-haired breeds, such as Labrador Retrievers, the presence of the dewclaws actually enhances the look of the ankle when looking down at the dog and for this reason the dewclaws are not usually removed. But in breeds where there is a wealth of feathering on the back of the leg concealing the dewclaw, and where the back of the leg has to receive regular combing, the dewclaw is best removed. Suffice to say, you would never find a Salador wearing dewclaws.

With the head and neck correctly positioned in natural repose and the left hand steadying the dog by being placed across the forechest, the right hand determines the correctness of the neck and shoulders.

ASSESSING SHOULDERS

With an open right hand, the shoulder blade is felt for with the thumb and first finger, above and in front of the elbow. The thumb should be able to detect the shoulder blade running backwards and sloping gradually at a nicely laid angle, with the hand gradually closing as the top of the shoulders are reached in a peak at the withers. Where the two shoulder blades meet at the withers, it should be impossible to get more than the forefinger to fit in the gap between the blades.

In a dog with an incorrect shoulder assembly it would be possible to get several fingers in easily between the blades, the result of which is that, in maturity, the dog is unfortunately adversely affected both in general appearance and in efficiency of movement. In time the muscle and fat gathers in the undesirable crevice between the expanded shoulder blades and the young dog's show career is soon over with what is termed 'loaded shoulders'. When standing, and particularly when moving around the show ring, the dog takes short, laboured strides and is unable to raise the top of the head much above the level of the back. A dog which has well-laid shoulders is more likely to have a good length of neck stretching from the back of the head down to the withers in a graceful arch. Such a dog moves around the ring with a high, aristocratic head carriage and takes effortless, even strides. In a dog which is correctly conditioned and exercised all its life, with the right amount of bodyweight, this highly desirable feature never disappears.

THE BODY

The middle piece of a Cavalier should incorporate a straight, short topline, with well-sprung ribs rippling beneath the palm and finger-tips as the hand is drawn backwards.

The combination of a good length of neck and a short, compact body is not always easy to achieve and the judge should give a lot of credit to the dog which possesses this rare combination. A dog with no spring of rib is termed 'slab-sided', and in the case of a male dog this fault remains with them for life. Curiously, in a female the condition can improve with maturity and certainly after having a litter in later life the ribs can spring out.

The ribs should be of good length and in balance with the individual dog, extending back to a short loin and, when viewing the dog from above and looking down on it, there should be a defined waistline from having no excess weight.

Incorrect:
Unbalanced, back
too long, dipping
topline, gay tail.

The pinbones should lie directly behind the loin at the top of the hind legs each side of the quarters and should only be just about detectable with the finger-tips in a correctly conditioned dog. If the pinbones cannot be felt, then the dog is just too fat! If too prominent and obvious then the individual dog is way below its correct bodyweight, even if it does not comply with the suggested weight standard of twelve to eighteen pounds. For humane reasons, thank goodness, this ruling has never been enforced at shows, where the experienced judges prefer to gauge the size of the ideal Cavalier with their eyes, not with the weight scales.

HINDQUARTERS

These should also be examined with the right hand. The first impressions are gained by closing the fingers and palm of the hand together on the back of the hind leg between the tail and the hock. The 'ham' of the hind leg should feel positively plump when squeezed, which indicates to the examiner that there is little wrong with the leg bone mechanics under the flesh. A dog with serious hip and knee joint abnormalities would have a different feel altogether. The hind leg would have a 'wasted' look, bony and flabby to the touch, which is a reflection of the lack of any real muscle tone as a result of the dog being unable to use itself correctly.

The thumb of the right hand should detect a graceful curve to the bend of the stifle back to the hock, where again the rest of the leg should drop down in a straight vertical line when viewed from the side or back. In this position, when the dog is viewed by the handler looking down over it and along the body lines, the points of the stifles should be just about visible and turned out slightly. This highly desirable feature is termed 'well-turned stifles'.

The lower joint of the hock reaching to the well-padded foot should be a short joint, and this feature, also highly desirable, gives the dog propulsion and drive when in motion. A straight stifle with no turn and a long lower joint gives the dog quite the opposite effect in movement. There is more likely to be a tendency to cow hocks when the dog is viewed moving away, and seen from the side the dog takes short, stilted strides. The overall effect is

STANDING STILL   **MOVING AWAY**

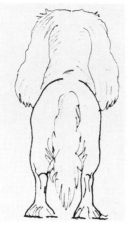

Correct: Hocks parallel to each other and perpendicular to the ground.

Incorrect: Hocks turning in and feet turning out. 'Hocky' and 'cow hocks' moving close behind.

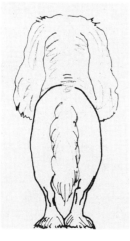
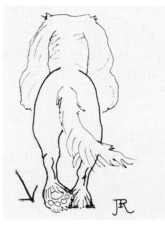

Incorrect: Hocks turning out and feet turning in.

not very attractive and any amount of exercising will unfortunately never alter the dog's appearance and movement.

The tail is naturally an extension of the spine and of the level of the topline and, when in motion, the tail should rise not much above the level of the dog's back and should be used in a way which reflects the breed's gaiety.

COAT
The whole dog should be clothed in a wealth of glossy coat, straight, and with a silky texture. The skin should be supple and clean with no dryness or scurf present, and the dog when nursed should have a wholesome and 'fresh outdoor' aroma about it.

MOVEMENT
The correct movement as described in the breed standard comes as a result of a combination of several things. Correct conformation is paramount in the dog who has been properly reared and exercised by its owner, but also, to a smaller but important extent, it is the dog's temperament and outlook on life, which is reflected in its movement.

Correct: Side movement, covering the ground with balanced strides. Good head and tail carriage.

Incorrect: 'Pacing'. The body rolls as the weight is shifted from side to side, as the legs are used incorrectly. The head is carried too low.

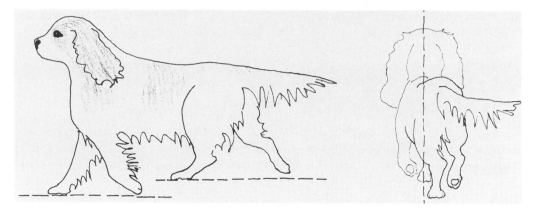

Incorrect: 'Crabbing'. Upright shoulder, correct angulation at rear. The dog swings its body out to compensate, resulting in the head being carried to the side. The front and rear movement are aligned on the slant, with stilted steps at the front.

TEMPERAMENT

The Cavalier King Charles Spaniel's temperament should, ideally, be neither nervous nor aggressive. Equally undesirable is the middle of the road individual which cannot make up its mind which of these things it wants to be, and just whines and barks all day long!

Despite all breeders' well-meaning endeavours to breed first-class specimens, the majority of their puppies end up in private pet homes where soundness and good temperament are the main essentials, and there is little objection to a tail in the air or a smudge on the face. It does not matter whether the dog is the best-looking in the world; if its temperament is all wrong then the owner is wasting not only their own time, but also the time of all unsuspecting breeders who use the dog in the show world, while in the case of a pet, the keeping of the dog ceases to be a hobby. Bad temperament is nearly always inherited and not acquired and should be a very important consideration when choosing breeding stock or a companion dog.

THE WHOLE PICTURE

Inexperienced but totally well-meaning judges will often look across the ring at a dog whose whole appearance strikes them in a very favourable way, without actually quite knowing why. In all probability it is because the dog is what is termed 'well-balanced'. Every piece is well made, the parts fitting in and flowing into one another, presenting an eye-catching outline.

The top grade and most experienced judges can see at a glance if the dog is a well-balanced one, but the practical way to check is easy. On the table, the dog's show lead can be gathered up and used as a measuring tape; the distance between the peak of the withers to the tail root should be the same as the distance from the same point to the bottom of the front pad resting on the table. If this is correct and if the dog is unexaggerated in the rest of its features when viewed overall, then all things being equal it can be safely termed well-balanced. With experience the novice judge hopefully soon develops an 'eye' for this from across the ring without any further, practical, investigation.

Looking at the ideal Cavalier King Charles Spaniel show dog, the head and eyes should display intelligence and attentiveness with the dog watching the handler's eyes and every move. The dog should stand well up on its toes, and should repose and move well when held on a loose lead. The ideal show dog should be supple and fit and ready to step off in whatever direction, engaging a well-balanced gait at a moment's indication from the handler. The dog should be fearless and stand its ground when approached either on the table or on the floor.

Combined with everything that is good about the breed, the last paragraph is the 'cherry on the cake', and such a dog is a very great pleasure to own and show.

Chapter Five

THE EARLY BREEDERS

From the 16th to 17th century the early Toy Spaniels flourished as much-loved pets of the ladies of the Court, from Tudor times until the Royal Stuarts reigned in England – King Charles II giving his name to the toy dogs which we know as King Charles Spaniels.

But as several Royal families showed their preference for and enthusiasm over the Royal Toy Spaniels, so another Royal dynasty was to change canine fashions. When the Dutch Court of William III came to power, the popularity of the Pug dog grew. These dogs were often portrayed being held by a little black page boy.

Although the Toy Spaniels fell from Royal favour, the Blenheim or Marlborough red and white spaniels remained firm favourites with the Dukes of Marlborough and the strain flourished at Blenheim Palace up until the early 1900s.

The English Kennel Club came into being in 1873 and with it came properly organised dog shows, breed clubs and the all-important Breed Standards. This era also brought new fashions and serious, dedicated breeders who preferred the flat face, high-domed head and the long set ears on their spaniels to the fine-faced or short-nosed types. This flat-faced type flourished and has continued to develop into what is now a superb and beautiful breed, known then, as it is now, as the King Charles Spaniel.

THE CAVALIER CATALYST

So far as the early history and development of the Cavalier King Charles Spaniel is concerned, what happened next provided more than one coincidence with the United States of America. In the early 1920s Roswell Eldridge from Saddle Rock, Long Island, New York, used to make several trips a year to England. He loved to ride to hounds with the West Somerset Hunt and he loved dogs, specifically the old type Toy Spaniels depicted in the old paintings. Eldridge, although coming from a poor family, was a self-made multi-millionaire, mainly from astute business deals. His desire was to acquire from England a breeding pair of King Charles Spaniels of the genuine Stuart era type. Sadly he was to be disappointed in his search but, undeterred, he placed an advertisement in the 1926 Crufts Dog Show Catalogue which must have been the most momentous and historical public appeal notice ever to revive an old breed. The advertisement read:

"Blenheim Spaniels of the Old Type, as shown in the pictures of Charles II's time, long face, no stop, flat skull, not inclined to be domed with spot in centre of skull. The 1st prizes of

£25 in class 947 and 948 are given by Roswell Eldridge Esq., New York, USA. Prizes to go to the nearest type required."

Roswell Eldridge was at that time almost seventy years old and even in his wildest dreams he could never have envisaged what his advertisement was going to lead to. Sadly he did not live to see the full outcome of the seed he had planted in the minds of the breeders who read that notice that day, but in any event his name will never be forgotten wherever Cavalier King Charles Spaniels are concerned.

AMICE PITT: TTIWEH LINE

July 4th marks an important day in American history and, by coincidence, Independence Day 1897 was the birth day of the lady who was to read Roswell Eldridge's advertisement and to be mainly instrumental in bringing his dreams to reality.

In Britain today all the different regional Cavalier King Charles Spaniel clubs take it in turn annually to stage a Rally to commemorate this lady's life and contribution to the breed. Their celebrations are in deep gratitude for her work and perseverance when, especially in the early pioneer days, she received little encouragement. The event is called the 'Amice Pitt Rally'.

Amice Pitt was the daughter of Sir Everett and Lady Millais and she appeared to have

Hentzau Sweet Nell (21.3.1927); Winner of the £25 Crufts prize in 1928.

'Dinah' (14.4.1927) – Belinda of Ttiweh: One of the 'Nosey' King Charles Spaniels bitches used in the late 1920s.

inherited her father's genius for breeding dogs. Sir Everett was a dedicated dog breeder, even qualifying at St Thomas's Hospital to obtain a medical degree to assist him in his work of reviving the 'Fino de Paris' type of Basset Hound, which became established in Britain in 1874. A talented family, Sir Everett was the son of the celebrated pre-Raphaelite painter, Sir John Millais.

Amice Pitt always had a deep interest in and love for dogs and horses, but her first love was for music and she was known for practising for five hours a day at the piano. However the First World War had a fateful effect on her life path and put paid to her desire to study music in Germany. Instead she spent some time on a cousin's farm in Norfolk, eventually married and acquired her name, Mrs Hewitt Pitt, from whence came her now famous prefix Ttiweh.

Her first love for dogs fell to Chow-Chows, but her mother, Lady Millais, owned a blenheim King Charles spaniel given to her by her daughter in 1924, and the two ladies decided to breed from her.

In order to find a suitable mate for her bitch who, after some difficulty, was registered as Waif Julia, Amice Pitt visited Miss Brunne, who owned the highly successful Hentzall King Charles Spaniels. It was during this visit that her attention was drawn to Roswell Eldridge's advertisement.

Amice Pitt's imagination must have certainly been fired in no uncertain manner when Waif Julia won Mr Eldridge's handsome prize of £25 for the Best Bitch of "The Old Type" at Crufts 1927, only a year after the challenge had been laid down!

GETTING ESTABLISHED
By the time Crufts Dog show came round again things had really started to get under way and, by now, a group of enthusiastic breeders were discussing the formation of a Club to revive the old-type spaniels. Miss Mostyn Walker became Chairman by the toss of a coin;

Ann's Son: The new Breed Standard was modelled on this dog.

The Young Pretender of Grenewich and Avril of Astondowns.

her dog Ann's Son had already won the £25 three times and he was eventually to become the dog upon whom the new Breed Standard was to be modelled. With a new Breed Standard came a new name 'Cavalier King Charles Spaniel' and, with Mrs Pitt as Secretary and a new committee, the first Breed club was formed in 1928. The events of those few years brought mixed emotions from the King Charles Spaniel breeders: some thought, or even hoped, that these new pioneer breeders were never going to succeed, others were glad to find an outlet for their long-nosed throw-outs.

A great deal of time and trouble had gone into doing away with the long nose by the King Charles Spaniel breeders, and they now had their own Breed Standard, so it was only natural that they should feel apprehensive. But by early 1929 the King Charles Spaniel breed correspondent conceded to *Dog World* readers that: "There is no doubt this Club has come to stay and we must admire their efforts, even if some of us do not agree with them." By that time, which was only three years after Roswell Eldridge's appeal, there was a Breed Standard recognised by the official Kennel Club, a Breed Club, and nine classes laid on at Crufts Dog Show for Cavalier King Charles Spaniels!

As with all worthwhile projects, nothing ever comes easily at first, and the new breeders were to meet with many uphill struggles, demoralising disappointments and setbacks. Large numbers of dogs had to be run on to see which produced the desired type, which in itself must have created a lot of work and expense, and little was recouped in puppy sales as most were given away to good homes. Even a show winner could only raise a few guineas, which was not a great deal of money even in those days.

Together with her Chow-Chows and Cavaliers, Mrs Pitt's kennel numbered sixty to eighty dogs, and with her daughter Jane, now Mrs Hugh Bowdler, she travelled the country exhibiting the Cavaliers in the 'Any Variety' classes, guaranteeing their own breed classes to encourage the show societies to promote more classes.

But by the early thirties even the great Mrs Pitt sounded a little disillusioned as she wrote: "I must confess that our living specimens are, in the majority of cases, falling very short of the Standard and are a great deal too big. The first class Cavalier is very hard to breed, but the few in existence have earned many admirers."

The coming of the Second World War dealt another blow to her for, apart from retaining three Cavalier bitches and one male, all her dogs had to be destroyed because of lack of food and suitable homes. Other kennels were also disbanded and yet many dogs survived in private homes. Many people would never have recovered from such a harrowing and traumatic experience and would have given up without much difficulty, but the event only fired Mrs Pitt with a more vigorous determination to succeed, and this she surely did!

STARTING AGAIN

After the war Mrs Pitt and many other breeders regrouped and went back as close as they could to the source – Ann's Son. Mrs Speedwell Massingham, who was well ahead with her Loyalty Way Cavaliers, wrote a lovely description of Ann's Son: "a toy spaniel of thirteen pounds, short in the back, entirely flat head, streaming ears to his legs, large dark eyes wide apart, nose long, tipped with jet to match his dark eyes, a white blaze running right up the forehead, thick soft silky coat marked red and silver blenheim, and sound as a bell. He was

supreme. I realise it is not only all the perfect points that gave him glory, it was the overall quality which this exquisite little dog had and which shone out of his face that made him Best Ever Born!"

Not far from Coppice House, where I write this book, lies the beautiful black and white timbered house known as Daywell Manor at Gobowen. All these years later it is still used as a pony stud, but it was the home of Lt. Col. and Mrs Lawrence Brierley, who were great pony lovers and breeders. When they died it was said that their ashes were scattered along their pony gallops. But despite being more involved with breeding ponies, they were to provide an important key dog so far as the Cavalier King Charles Spaniel breeders were concerned.

On October 7th 1945 the Brierleys bred a very important Cavalier King Charles Spaniel litter indeed. They had mated their blenheim bitch Daywell Nell to the ruby dog Cannonhill Richey. Daywell Nell was the result of mating Ann's Son back to his own daughter Miss Ann's Son, who in turn was

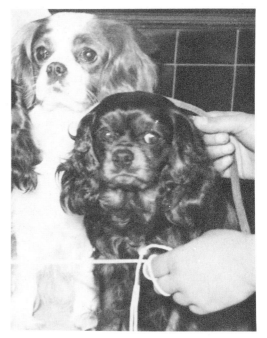

The first dog and bitch Champions, made up in the late 1940s, Ch. Daywell Roger and Ch. Amanda Loo of Ttiweh. This pair would not look out of place in the show ring today.

out of Nightie Nightie by Duke's Son by Ann's Son again! This breeding programme in itself must have said a lot about the genetic soundness and the stamina of the original breeding stock.

MRS JENNINGS' PLANTATION LINE

Cannonhill Richey was a popular stud dog amongst the early breeders and he was predominantly Mrs Jennings' Plantation bloodlines. She had always owned a King Charles Spaniel from childhood, until the coming of the First World War left her without a dog. In 1926 her husband, whilst attending a business meeting, was told by a colleague that his wife wanted to find a home for a King Charles Spaniel bitch. So Mr Jennings bought the bitch for his wife. She turned out to be a genuine product and descendant of the Marlborough Spaniels and was called Blenheim Palace Poppet. In the litter born at Daywell Manor was a blenheim dog who was to have a profound influence on the development of the Cavalier King Charles Spaniel. In the same year as his birth, 1945, the Kennel Club agreed to a separate registration for the newly revived breed.

By a stroke of luck Mrs Pitt heard about this dog and bought him unseen for her daughter Jane. He was registered Daywell Roger and was affectionately known as "Lou". During his long life of twelve years plus, he sired eleven Champions as well as being, in 1948, the first Cavalier King Charles Spaniel to gain a Champion's title. It cannot be emphasised enough that the appearance of a dog who looked like this so early in the proceedings was quite extraordinary, and Ch. Daywell Roger was a remarkable dog who was far ahead of his time.

Ch. Daywell Roger won the Top Stud Dog award from 1951 to 1954 inclusive and, as a show dog, his breed type, balance and all-round soundness found him favour with breed specialists and all-rounder judges equally well – always a sign of a good dog!

Another important purchase by Mrs Pitt was a blenheim bitch from Mrs Katie Eldred, a resident of Canada who had previously lived in the USA. The bitch was first registered as

The extraordinary head and breed type shown by Ch. Daywell Roger.

Ch. Little Dorritt of Ttiweh (14.11.1945) with her litter by Ch. Daywell Roger (24.8.1945), which included the influential stud dogs Ch. Jupiter of Ttiweh and Mars of Ttiweh.

The first Cavalier KC Championship Show, August 1946. Judge Mrs Jennings, Katie Eldred (left) with Bitch CC and BOB Belinda of Saxham, and Jane Pitt (now Bowdler) with Daywell Roger, Dog CC.

Lady Jane of Turnworth, but in those days the Kennel Club allowed the change of a dog's name if desired, and Mrs Pitt chose to re-register the bitch as Little Dorrit of Ttiweh. She became a champion in 1950 and had a similar combination of bloodlines to Ch. Daywell Roger, with Plantation and Ann's Son breeding. The union of Roger to Little Dorritt produced Ch. Harmony of Ttiweh, who was the first Cavalier to win a Best in Show, at a Toy Dog Show in 1951. In a repeat litter came the brothers Ch. Jupiter of Ttiweh and Mars of Ttiweh – the latter was considered the better stud dog, although Jupiter was outstanding for glamour.

The first Championship show was held at Stratford-upon-Avon on August 29th 1946 with Mrs Jennings as the judge. Twenty-eight Cavaliers, making one hundred and nine entries, were entered and Best in Show was won by the seven-year-old blenheim bitch, Mrs Katie Eldred's Belinda of Saxham, dam of Ch. Little Dorrit. Belinda was highly thought of and considered to be on a par with the quality of Ann's Son, only the War prevented her gaining a title. The young Daywell Roger was the Best Dog, handled by Jane Bowdler.

ABOVE: Mrs Amice Pitt, Mrs Pares-Wilson (later Lady Daniel – Cocklehill) and Mrs Helen Pilkington.

BELOW: Vera Rennie and Mme Harper Trois Fontaines.

Daphne Murray with Fickle of Ttiweh (21.8.1947) – dam of Ch. Raoul of Ttiweh.

The appealing type of Ch. Hillbarn Alexander of Ttiweh, an early, influential stud dog, born 26.4.1947.

SOME PROMINENT POST-WAR LINES

Maud Sawkins's Grenewich King Charles Spaniels were well in evidence during the late thirties, remaining independent of the Ann's Son line. Her important blenheim dog, the Young Pretender of Grenewich, was born in 1944 and figures well in the early pedigrees of successful dogs under the ownership of Miss Phyllis Mayhew of the Minshang prefix and her sister, Joyce Green of Heatherside Cavaliers; also the Hillbarn dogs of Helen Pilkington (not to be confused with Elise Pilkington of the Goldicote Cavaliers).

Mrs Green's early champions, litter brother and sister Heatherside Andrew and Anthea, were by The Young Pretender mated to Ch. Daywell Roger's litter sister Daywell Amber, Andrew becoming Top Stud Dog in 1955 and winning the Cup for the Best Head twice under Mrs Pitt and daughter Jane Bowdler. In fact many of the early champions were a combination of Ch. Daywell Roger's breeding and The Young Pretender of Grenewich, a recipe which seemed to work.

The prefix 'De Fontenay' also figures well in those early Cavalier pedigrees, and belonged to the colourful character of Mme J. Harper Trois-Fontaines, who was perhaps more noted for her celebrated Pyrenean Mountain dogs. Nevertheless a small nucleus of her breeding stock, based on Plantation and Ttiweh bloodlines, were to provide the sound basis for several other important breeders of that era.

Although she had lost interest in Cavaliers by the early fifties, Mme Harper Trois-Fontaines made a valuable contribution to the breed and will be remembered for looking after valuable breeding stock during the war, where others found it necessary to disband or destroy their dogs.

The 'De Fontenay' bloodlines figure well behind Vernon Green's Astondown line and Helen Pilkington's Hillbarn Cavaliers. Her Hillbarns were nearly always tricolours, the colour that she favoured and is mostly associated with, so it was possible to acquire a very nice blenheim from her. Amice Pitt's blenheim dog Ch. Hillbarn Alexander of Ttiweh was a very successful show and stud dog for her and was one of the key sires of that time. For the home kennel, Mrs Pilkington's tricolour Ch. Hillbarn Quixote by Ch. Heatherside Andrew became Top Stud Dog in 1963.

Mrs Pilkington's stalwart loyalty towards one colour reminds me so much in part of Mary Roslin-Williams, the famous judge and breeder of the black Mansergh Labrador Retrievers, who would never be seen dead with anything but a black Labrador on the end of the lead! One yellow bitch puppy, who did escape the early cull while her breeder was away from home, became the very beautiful Ch. Poolstead Mary Rose, raised by the famous Poolstead Kennels of Mrs R. V. Hepworth in Cheshire.

As some breeders become associated with one colour, so another early Cavalier breeder, Vera Rennie, yearned to win with another colour other than the whole colours she was more associated with. Her black and tan dog Ch. Royalist of Veren was a key dog and a direct predecessor to the male line of the most successful wholecolour family of Cavaliers who exist today.

The day Mrs Rennie won her first CC with a blenheim was, she said, the happiest day of her life; but, sadly, it proved to be her last, for in all the excitement she collapsed and died outside the secretary's office at Birmingham City championship show held in Handsworth

Like Ch. Daywell Roger, Britta White's Ch. Raoul of Ttiweh (7.10.1951) was an extraordinary looking dog, far ahead of his time.

RIGHT: Ch. Prologue of Ttiweh (31.1.1950): Tricolour type of the early 1950s.

BELOW: Eight Champions pictured in 1954 (left to right): Ch. Comfort of Ttiweh, Ch. Trilby of Ttiweh, Ch. Jupiter of Ttiweh, Ch. Amanda Loo of Ttiweh, Ch. Little Dorritt of Ttiweh, Ch. Daywell Roger, Ch. Harmony of Ttiweh, Ch. Hillbarn Alexander of Ttiweh.

Ch. Abelard of Ttiweh (10.10.1950): An influential stud dog who 'fixed' beautiful necks and shoulders into the early Cavaliers, pictured with a Pug dog – the breed who ousted Royal Toy Spaniels from Royal favour in the reign of William III.

Helen Pilkington's Hillbarn Cavaliers, pictured in the early 1950s.

Park. As a new decade followed the forties, the aforementioned kennels laid firm foundations for the breeders who followed them. Daphne Murray's Crustadele Cavaliers, with their rich Mediterranean-sounding names, gave much to the breed by way of lovely breed type. Being Katie Eldred's sister, Mrs Murray's early days were spent with her mentor, Mrs Pitt, assisting with the Ttiweh Chows and Cavaliers. Mrs Murray's bitch Ch. Piccola of Crustadele became the first-ever ruby champion in breed history in 1969.

Dumfries 1962: Amice Pitt with Ch. Cerdric of Ttiweh and Barbara Keswick's Pargeter Melissa, Best of Breed, judged by Beryl Sadler (Dendy).

BARBARA KESWICK'S PARGETER LINE

With the early fifties came a kennel which did much to influence the breed as it is today and which provided dogs who were firm foundations for many modern-day British breeders and overseas kennels, specifically those in America, Canada, Australia and New Zealand. Mrs Barbara Keswick's early Pargeters had close associations with those 'early greats', Champions Roger and Royalist, The Young Pretender and the pre-eminent Ttiwehs. Beryl Sadler's Ch. Abelard of Ttiweh, bred by Mrs Pitt, was to sire Barbara Keswick's great blenheim dog, Ch. Pargeter Bob Up, still revered by breeders today as one of the most beautiful Cavaliers ever. In 1961 he won the CC at Crufts under Mrs Joyce Green and won the CC three years running from the same year at the Cavalier King Charles Spaniel Club show.

Ch. Pargeter Bob Up sired four champions but, curiously, never won a Top Stud Dog award although he was such a superior Cavalier. It was to be his son, International Ch. Pargeter McBounce, out of the Ch. Cerdric of Ttitweh daughter Ch. Pargeter Melissa, who won the coveted stud dog award in 1973 and 1974 by virtue of his eight champion offspring. Mrs Keswick was greatly missed when she died in 1969, having been the driving force behind the Scottish Cavalier King Charles Spaniel Club. Some of her dogs, including McBounce, went to live with Miss Caroline Gatherall, who handled many of the Pargeters to success and whose lines were carried on in the Kershope Cavaliers. There was also Mrs Keswick's other 'right-hand man' in the person of Barbara Wall, who lovingly cared for the Pargeters from the nest to adulthood.

There were several other breeders who successfully combined their breeding activities with the different Cavalier Clubs' administration duties. The West of England Cavalier Club was the concept of Mrs Burroughes, whose Vairire prefix figured so closely behind many great dogs and bloodlines in the Cavalier world, although she was originally a King Charles Spaniel breeder from the 1940s. She bred, among others, Ch. Vairire Osiris, Ch. Vairire Charmaine of Crisdig and Vairire Venetia of Crisdig in the late fifties to early sixties, dogs whose names have a magical ring to more than a few people.

The Cavalier King Charles Spaniel Show 1963: Mrs Frank Cryer with Ch. Amelia of Laguna, judge Joe Braddon and Barbara Keswick's Ch. Pargeter Bob Up, handled by Caroline Gatheral.

1963: Julie Douglas and Ch. Vairire Osiris, judge Susan Burgess, and Evelyn Booth with Ch. Millstone Alleluia of Sunninghill.

The Cavalier King Charles Spaniel Club had Mr Stenning as Chairman and Year Book editor for some time, and his wife Eilidh bred the champion father and son, Ch. Cherrycourt Wake Robin and Ch. Cherrycourt Patrick of Maxholt, from chiefly Ttiweh and Pargeter bloodlines.

BREEDERS OF THE FIFTIES AND SIXTIES

Although she owned other colours, it was chiefly Peggy Talbot's dominant strain of tricolour Cavaliers who were to bring her fame with her Maxholt prefix. Her early dogs were closely interlinked with Irene Booth's Bowstones, Vera Preece's Chandlers and Mrs Mark Patten's Barings Cavaliers.

Her noted tricolour Minstrel Boy of Maxholt was to win her Top Stud Dog awards for 1975 and 1977, chiefly by his magical liaisons with Ch. Cherrycourt Patrick children. Mrs Virginia Barwell's close associations with Mrs Talbot were reflected in her own success with her Charlottetown Cavaliers, the prefix being taken from the famous thoroughbred racehorse whom Virginia cared for while in Captain Boyd-Rochfort's stables.

Southern Counties 1963: Evelyn Booth with Ch. Millstone Barings Margareta, judge Pamela Turle, Sheila Halsall with Ch. Edward of Knightlow, who won the Crufts Dog CC in 1963 and 1964.

Pamela Turle's prefix Sunninghill was first noticed in 1949 and she has her own special place in different chapters of this book. In the early fifties her great tricolour stud dog, Ch. Aloysius of Sunninghill, sired the tricolour bitch Ch. My Fair Lady of Eyeworth, one of the first champions for Lady Mary Forwood, a well-known personality and wife of Sir Dudley Forwood. Lady Forwood's black and tan dog Ch. Cointreau of Eyeworth played an important part in the pedigrees of modern-day whole colours, but in many people's opinion her blenheim dog, Ch. Archie McMuck of Eyeworth, was considered her best.

LITTLEBREACH AND CHACOMBE LINES

On the death of Helen Pilkington's husband, Barbara Percival took her cousin's Hillbarn Cavaliers and extended her kennel of already successful Little Breach Basenjis and Dachshunds. Her blenheim dog Ch. Dickon of Little Breach has earned his visual place in several books on the Breed by his all-round excellence. Ch. Venetia of Littlebreach was owned by Diane Schilizzi, whose particolour Chacombe Cavaliers benefited from Mrs Percival's bloodlines, just as her whole colours promoted Molly Marshall's Kormar breeding. Mrs Schilizzi's bitch, Ch. Chacombe Camilla was the first ruby to win Best of Breed at Crufts, in 1978.

Another breeder to favour Littlebreach and Chacombe lines was Joan Winters, with her Kentonvilles; her first Cavalier was by Miss Mayhew's Ch. Minshang Sir Roger. Mrs Dallas Archer based her Jia kennel on Littlebreach, Bowstones and Crisdig lines. Her lovely blenheim bitch Ch. Jia Egeria and full blenheim brother, Mr and Mrs Newton's Ch. Jia Laertes of Tonnew, were outstanding. Ch. Laertes was a handsome and regal-looking male who captured the hearts of many the day he swept around the ring at Crufts in 1981, winning the Toy Group in some style, so ably shown off by his owner, Margaret Newton.

Of course the first Cavalier to win the Toy Group at Crufts in 1963 and to carve her place in history, was Ch. Aloyius of Sunninghill's blenheim daughter, Mrs Frank Cryers' Ch. Amelia of Laguna, followed in another ten years by Messrs Hall and Evans, Ch. Alansmere Aquarius. Almost twenty years later these breeders were to repeat their win, with Ch. Spring Tide of Alansmere, another blenheim male, in 1994. The only other member of this elite group of Cavaliers to date who has won the Crufts Toy Group was Mrs Wiggins' tricolour male, Whyteplace Apollo in 1990, although several others have come very close.

THE START OF THE SALADOR LINE

Without leaving the late fifties, I must make mention of the breeder whose kennel I first went to in the early seventies for a stud dog and who was recommended to me by Sheila Halsall, who sold me my first Cavalier, Pantisa Christmas Carol. What a portentous visit that turned out to be.

The first thing I noticed that day, as I walked into Barbara Palfree's veterinary surgery in Derby, was a painting on the wall of a tricolour Cavalier with a superb head. The glorious eyes and expression, the pure white muzzle and mahogany tan, just the great head pattern, bowled me over. When I learned that it was a painting of a living dog – well, I could hardly contain my excitement. Blagreaves Bengamino of Ttiweh, a male heavily linebred to Mrs Pitt's dogs, was a dog who set me up for a lifetime, as, to this day, his tricolour descendants in my kennel remain so true to his type and image.

As a veterinary practitioner, Miss Palfree's duties prevented her from fully participating in the show aspect of Cavaliers, although she served as Chairman of the Northern Cavalier Club for many years. She did make up the tricolour bitch Ch. Josephine of Blagreaves, sired by Ch. Barings Fortescue, son of Ch. Aloyius, and Josephine is the Cavalier on whom the Beswick china dog is modelled. Her tricolour dog Bonnyglen Jasper of Blagreaves, bred by Kathleen Yoxall, was to sire, amongst others, the Coaker family's Ch. Homeranne Andy Capp, a dominant sire in the late seventies.

I liked Miss Palfree very much and well remember the last evening I spent with her. She was terribly interesting to listen to and whenever she said anything profound her eyes used to vanish into her forehead! Each time I rose from my chair to go home she kept filling my sherry glass, and I never did remember which route I took to come home from Derby that

*Barbara Palfree
with a group of
Blagreaves
Cavaliers.*

night. Sadly, it was the last time I ever saw her. That American gentleman, Roswell Eldridge, would have been inordinately proud to have seen what his advertisement, displayed in 1926, was to bring about in the first thirty years – and perhaps a little bit proud indeed that, in the sixties, there was to come a fellow American who was to breed in England 'A Dog of Dogs'.

Chapter Six

A DOG OF DOGS

There must be many romantic stories concerning Cavalier King Charles Spaniels over the centuries – how people came to own them by chance and how famous dogs came to be in existence. There have been many key dogs who have enabled the history and the development of the breed to unravel, but one romantic story, which culminated in a 'Dog of Dogs' being born, stands out from amongst many.

In Shropshire, across the lush meadows and leafy lanes from my old home, Coppice House, lies Halston Hall, which is north east of Oswestry and now the home of Major Harvey. Halston was the home of a great field trialling lady and Golden Retriever owner, Mrs Patience Eccles.

In the spring of 1959 she had bred a litter of Cavalier King Charles Spaniel puppies by the blenheim Ch. Raoul of Ttiweh to the black and tan bitch Rhea of Eyeworth, and her neighbours, the Kynastons at nearby Hardwick Hall, acquired one of the puppies.

American-born Gertrude Biddle and her husband came up from the West Country to their relatives the Kynastons and became very taken with their new puppy. So much so, that Mrs Biddle's husband presented her with the puppy's litter sister as a birthday gift – and what a wonderful acquisition she turned out to be!

The puppy became Ch. Roulette of Temple Hill, and she became not only a great show bitch, winning her last CC at nine years and so proving what a laster she was, but was also the foundation of the Ottermouths and of a great dynasty of dogs. Mrs Biddle was a wonderful example of a small breeder who bred very few litters of puppies but still managed to leave a lasting influence on the breed through her dogs. If any puppies were unsold in their early life they remained with the family as household pets. Mrs Biddle described Roulette as the family's 'Dog of a lifetime' in every way.

Over the years well-known breeders gave her more dogs, which she reared and campaigned to their titles. From Mr and Mrs Bradley-Reynolds came Ch. Bredonvale Bernard and Ch. Ttiweh Roseanne came from Mrs Pitt; but most importantly Ch. Crisdig Geordie of Ottermouth was another wonderful present from her husband, this time to commemorate a wedding anniversary! Bred by Susan Burgess, Geordie was, in due course, mated to Roulette, producing the litter sisters Reinette and Rosette.

When mated to Bacarole of Crustadele, Reinette bred two champion blenheim males in Ring a Ding and the very glamorous Requiem of Ottermouth. Most importantly, when

ABOVE: Ch. Rose Mullion of Ottermouth: A sire of far-reaching influence, owned by Gertrude Biddle.

RIGHT: The glamorous Ch. Requiem of Ottermouth, owned by Gertrude Biddle.
                    Photo: Anne Roslin Williams.

Gertrude Biddle's Ch. Roulette of Temple Hill and Ch. Crisdig Geordie of Ottermouth.

Blackpool 1970: Lady Mary Forewood with Ch. Archie McMuck of Eyeworth, judge Evelyn Booth, and Sheila Halsall with Ch. Gleamer of Pantisa – two outstanding Cavaliers of the late sixties.

Richmond 1974: John Evans and Ch. Bredonvale Mirabelle, judge Diane Schilizzi, and Heather Ferday with Rhosnesney Prince Ivan of Rhybank – two Cavaliers who were of great influence.

Caroline Compston's Gillies Farne Silver Shadow of McGoogans: An influential son of Ch. Rose Mullion of Ottermouth.

Rosette was bred to Ch. Vairire Osiris, she produced the champion blenheim brother and sister Rose Mullion and Rose Mary. When bred back to Mrs. Burgess's Ch. Crisdig Harlequin, Rose Mary produced the tricolour dog Ch. Ottermouth Back Badge; but it was her brother who was to become one of the breed's legendary sires.

ROSE MULLION

Rose Mullion, who shared the same call name of 'Pickle' as his sire Osiris, was not only a great sire himself, with seven champion children, but he turned out to be a dog with a far-reaching influence. His stud career culminated in winning the Top Stud dog award in 1976 and he was a successful show dog in his own right too. He was not as heavily campaigned as some, through being in the same kennel as Ch. Requiem, but even so, he was a Toy Group winner, won Best of Breed at Crufts and was shortlisted in the Toy Group and won Best in Show at a Breed Speciality championship show.

A sire of sires, Rose Mullion's sons inherited his prepotent influence even though they were from varied bitch lines, and many a great kennel was given a great injection of blue blood after using this dog. Rose Mullion passed on his outstanding glamour, lovely eyes, black nose pigment and rich blenheim coat plus his all round soundness to his descendants, who were to create what was to be 'A never-ending story'. In alphabetical order, Rose Mullion's influential sons were: Ch. Bredonvale Bernard, Farne Silver Shadow of McGoogans, Kindrum Roulette, Ronnoc True Luck, Rosemar Ulysses of Leynsord and Ch. Rosemerryn of Alansmere. They and their sire were blessed with longevity, many of them living well into their teens, which is a very important consideration in the Cavalier as a breed.

When one looks back into Rose Mullion's pedigree it is not difficult to understand why he was such a stud force: his breeding was immaculate and he had a 'Stud dog's pedigree'. Rose Mullion was the culmination of the products of some great kennels and breeders.

In Ch. Daywell Roger and Ch. Raoul of Ttiweh alone we have two dogs who were way ahead of their time. Amice Pitt just about summed up Rose Mullion when she wrote to Mrs Biddle after seeing him again at a show in later life. Rose Mullion was making a rare appearance and had just won Best in Show under Daphne Murray at the West of England Cavalier Championship show. Mrs Pitt wrote: "How lovely I thought Rose Mullion looked – it was lovely to look at such an outstanding dog – all class and presence."

CH. HOMARANNE CAPTION

At the Cavalier King Charles Spaniel Club championship show in the spring of 1977 Mrs Pitt was to send another prophetic message of encouragement from the ringside to the owners of a very wayward blenheim dog puppy who had just been placed third in his class and was doing his best not to win! Sadly Mrs Pitt was never to see the fulfilment of the destiny of the puppy who had caught her eye. He was to become Ch. Homaranne Caption, owned by Molly Coaker and bred by daughter Anne.

In thoroughbred horse racing circles they reckon that the three names that most frequently come up in conversation are those of Northern Dancer, Secretariat and Mr Robert Sangster. In the Cavalier world their equivalents, the three most uttered names, would be Ch. Rose Mullion of Ottermouth, Ch. Homaranne Caption and Molly Coaker!

Caption was surely a dog born by a quirk of fate, because a mating had already been planned between his sire, Homerbrent Henry and Ch. Homerbrent Captivations's daughter Candida, but Candida was only a few days into her heat when Arkle of Homerbrent had already helped himself to her. As Homerbrent Henry was shortly due to leave England for Australia to join Betty Reading, his fate was that he was mated to Ch. Homerbrent

Molly Coaker with Ch. Homaranne Caption.

Captivation instead, and Caption was in the litter of four puppies.

Homerbrent Henry was sired by Rose Mullion's son Ch. Bredonvale Bernard, who would have become a great stud force in his own right had he not had to watch all the best 'girls' visiting his father, and Henry was already following suit by siring three English Champions from a few litters prior to his departure to Australia, where he subsequently won his title.

In the beginnings of the powerful Homerbrent kennel, based in South Devon, Mrs Biddle's home was to be a favourite source for stud dogs and the very first Homerbrent champion was Rose Mullion's daughter Lindy Lou in 1972, quickly followed by Ch. Homerbrent Minstrel, son of Ch. Requiem of Ottermouth, from bitches firmly based on Susan Burgess's Crisdig line.

My personal all-time favourite of the Homerbrents would be the classical blenheim bitch Ch. Homerbrent Samantha, whose parents were by Ch. Requiem of Ottermouth and Ch. Crisdig Geordie of Ottermouth, and grand-daughter to one of the Coaker family's first Cavaliers, Harrowbeer Unity, bred by Mary Kiser.

But without doubt the Coakers' greatest stud dog was Ch. Homaranne Caption – and a great show dog in his own right, winning thirteen CCs and three Toy Groups during his career. 'Caper' had the look of a great stud dog and stamped his looks on his stock with his superb breed type, distinctive head pattern, classical outline, rich blenheim coat colouring and his great ring presence. A much talked-about stud dog, perhaps, but there was no getting away from it, in possessing the ability to put actual champions into the show ring, Caption had no peers. His sixteen title holders made him the joint record holder for the overall Toy Group. His stud dog achievements won Caption the Top Stud dog award from 1980 to 1986 inclusive, previous to which his half-brother Ch. Homaranne Andy Capp, also out of Ch. Homerbrent Captivation, had won the same accolade from 1978 to 1979. Since then Caption's double grandson, Ch. Homerbrent Carnival, has kept up the family's traditions by winning the same award two years running.

A long-lived dog, Caption passed away just after his fifteenth birthday. His last appearance in the show ring was in the Veteran class at Crufts in 1988, aged twelve and a half, and judged by Ireland's Amy Nugent. As Caption took the First prize in a class full of legendary old dogs, the watching crowd showed their appreciation of him and gave 'Caper' a great ovation.

SUSAN BURGESS: CRISDIG LINE

The West Country has always been a stronghold for great Cavalier King Charles Spaniels and their breeders, one of the foremost being Susan Burgess with her Crisdigs, so well supported by her late husband, Brigadier Jack Burgess.

'Romance and quirks of fate' would hardly be the immediate words that spring to mind when one thinks of the origins of her dogs, which were, indeed, more the result of carefully thought out plans and honest-to-goodness methodical stockmanship on her part. A really great breeder is classed as one who not only produces high-class dogs on a regular basis from their own kennel, but one whose dogs have the ability to blend in with and enhance other breeders' lines in a highly influential and lasting way over a long period of time.

Apart from Mrs Pitt, who scored one champion dog more than the twenty-seven in the

Susan Burgess with Ch. Crisdig Celebration, judge Pamela Turle, and Betty Miller with Ch. Otterholt Cold Cream.

records, Susan Burgess must surely rank as one of the great Cavalier breeders of all time. Her Crisdigs were the real McCoy – the classical type. Where fashions come and fashions go, the Crisdigs have had the capacity to remain an evergreen type which has had an enduring and unique appeal. Based on two half-sisters bred from the Vairire kennel of another great West Country breeder, Mrs Burroughes, the Crisdigs can be proud of their impressive and unbroken line of dog champions, all successful show and stud dogs in their own right – from the well-named Ch. Crisdig Celebration, Top Stud dog for three years from 1966 to 1968, to his son Ch. Crisdig Merry Matelot, who won the same award in 1971, down through Ch. Crisdig Leading Seaman and Ch. Crisdig Ted, to the youngest, Ch. Robinson of Crisdig. The many photographs in this book of first class Cavaliers pertaining to Susan Burgess' Crisdigs stand as splendid evidence of her endeavours within the breed.

MISS PAMELA TURLE: SUNNINGHILL

An affix closely figuring at the source of the Vairire and Crisdig pedigrees and interwoven with that of Mrs Pitt's Ttiwehs, is the name of Sunninghill, belonging to Pamela Turle, one of our oldest and most respected breeders.

These days Miss Turle spends her years of retirement at her secluded Monmouthshire farmhouse, her windows overlooking a beautiful and picturesque valley. In her heyday her contemporaries viewed her as a bit of a 'Golden' girl, and she became a pillar of the breed through her excellence as a breeder and as a judge. She not only bred and had very good Cavaliers but, as a judge, her opinion was much sought after, simply because she knew what the dogs were supposed to look like! Her forthright and unbiased approach to judging was much appreciated and, to my mind, on a good day's judging, her line up and understanding of 'blenheim type' was unrivalled.

In the late forties Miss Turle decided she wanted a small dog which she could take to the office and in 1949 she settled on a Cavalier bitch of all Ttiweh lines from Mrs Pitt and she was registered Lucasta of Sunninghill. In her early life Miss Turle had serious notions of becoming a film director, and a very good one she would have been too, but when Lucasta

*Pamela Turle's
Ch. Aloysius of
Sunninghill: Sire of
eight Champions
and winner of 19
CCs.*

won Miss Turle her very first CC she became really bitten with the bug and fate luckily made her a 'director' in another direction – that of Cavalier King Charles Spaniels. She did not have to wait long for her 'great' dog to come to her, although, at the time, she was not aware of him straightaway until, as she said: "It had dawned on my unpractised eye."

When Miss Turle's godson, Grant Wilson, brought Lucasta's daughter, Louisa, to Amulet of Sunninghill, the resulting litter produced Aloysius of Sunninghill, who was a heavily marked tricolour, and initially he was picked out by Miss Turle because of his sweet head and delightful Cavalier temperament.

Besides his heavily marked coat, Aloysius was by no means a small dog, and as, in Yorkshire, they would have described him as being a dog who was 'full measure', so Miss Turle's initial intentions were to let him go as a pet. Fortunately for the history of the breed, the only man who turned up to buy Aloysius turned him down – and he could have bought him for only eight guineas. So Aloysius remained at Sunninghill, where his eventful path in life opened up for him and his – by now – highly appreciative owner.

The sweet puppy head became a very beautiful adult head, a curious phenomenon with heavily marked tricolours, and his excellent conformation and exceptional movement were well apparent. During his long and illustrious twelve-year life as a show and stud dog, not only did 'Georgie' become Top Stud dog from 1959 to 1962 inclusive by virtue of his nine champion children, but the nineteen CCs that he won became the record for nearly forty years. Not until 1994 did Messrs Hall and Evans' blenheim dog Ch. Spring Tide of Alansmere, who is still being exhibited, amass twenty-four CCs and break the record.

Aloysius's sire Amulet was Top Sire 1957 and 1958 and, during Aloysius's early adulthood, Miss Turle tried to persuade prospective stud customers to follow the elementary study of breeding principles by advising them to use the sire who had produced the 'star'. But, as became apparent to Miss Turle and the owner/breeders of other dominant male lines, when one taps into the prepotent male family roots, such as the ones discussed in this book, it really does not matter which dog is used; they each turn out to be almost as good as one another. Indeed, one of Aloysius's champion progeny was the influential International Ch. Sunninghill Perseus of Lochfee, the sire of brood bitches behind the beginnings of the Crisdigs and of the McGoogans kennel of Mr and Mrs Gillies.

Their Ch. McGoogans Ruari became Top Stud dog in 1969 to 1970, chiefly by his record-setting daughter, Messrs Hall and Evans' Ch. Alansmere McGoogans Maggie May, whose fifteen CCs kept her as the bitch record holder until 1994. She was emulated by another blenheim bitch, Messrs Rix and Berry and Mrs Sylvia Lymer's Ch. Lymrey Top of the Pops, with nineteen CCs, who is still being exhibited. When mated to Rose Mullion's sire, Ch. Vairire Osiris, Maggie May bred Messrs Hall and Evans' blenheim dog Ch. Alansmere Aquarius, who is still not only the sole Cavalier King Charles Spaniel, but the only dog of Toy breed to win Supreme Best in Show at Crufts, which he achieved in 1973.

John Evans always felt that Ch. Vairire Osiris was underestimated as a stud dog, but Osiris hardly had anything to prove after siring Rose Mullion and Aquarius, and his sire was the influential Ch. Cerdric of Ttiweh, Top Stud dog for 1964 and 1965.

SALADOR CHARLOCK

To breed and own a prepotent stud dog is an immensely satisfying feeling, and only those people who have had one given to them by the gods will know quite what I mean.

Like those other fortunate owners, I did not have many years to wait for my first great dog to come to me. Initially I was rather disappointed when Salador Crumpet whelped her litter to Ch. Caderyn Black Tulip at Plas Cerrig Cottage, my former home in Llanymynech, only because my long-hoped-for black and tan bitch was not amongst the seven puppies.

Judy Watts, Black Tulip's owner, was as fascinated by the litter of all four coloured puppies as I was and she did, in fact, offer me a goodly sum for the blenheim bitch with a lozenge, Salador Cherrybird, plus a free stud to Black Tulip. But I know exactly what John Evans means when he says he knows he has bred himself a "good'un" by the excited tingling sensation on the back of his neck. I had such a sensation when Cherrybird popped out of the bitch, the last born of a well-marked litter – talk about beginner's luck! I knew then that I must never sell her. But the puppy that really did draw my eyes every time I went past the whelping box was a black and tan dog. The head, neck and shoulders stood out from the start: he really was a regal-looking individual.

As Charlock and Cherrybird started to get around, a little temporary disappointment set in when I invited my good friend, Ann Wallett-Evans, famous for her Poirot Rottweilers, to come into the garden to see my two pups as she was an expert on 'black and tans'. After a few minutes she exclaimed: "Well, you can't keep him...look at his front!" Personally I

Salador Charlock, owned by Sheila Smith. This dog was not widely used at stud, but he had a tremendous impact on the breed.

Anne Roslin-Williams.

wasn't looking at his front as I couldn't see past his beautiful head. However, I did ask Judy Watts about it and she reassured me that the fronts on black and tans needed time. She was so right, because Salador Charlock ended up with a perfect front. The seeming slackness in the pasterns was, I think now, more of an optical illusion, accentuated by the tufts of black puppy hair sprouting on the side of the tan forelegs.

Thereafter and over the years, whenever I used to invite Ann to come and look at black and tan puppies, I used to say jokingly: "What do you think about the fronts?" Her quick reply always was: "I seem to think we have had this conversation before!" Having faith in one's own dog is a very important thing and both Judy and I had faith in Charlock; in fact we quickly formed a friendship, chiefly because we were both tuned in to the same wavelength and had a mutual love and interest in horses, besides dogs.

Salador Charlock was hardly used by the breeders in the beginning. I think they were very suspicious of his broken coloured pedigree – a black and tan sire to a tricolour bitch. However, they liked his looks and he won over forty first prizes in breed classes. Curiously many of his children reverted back to becoming wholecolour dominant again – that is to say, they only produced whole colours of whatever coloured partner they were mated to. 'Whisky', as he was known, had mated three bitches by the time he was three years old, producing, amongst others, one puppy who became a Crufts Champion, the ruby bitch Salador Coppergleam. In fact one of his first and one of his last litters threw one up, the last being Ch. Rheinvelt Ringold V. Salador, Crufts Best of Breed in 1989. As an old dog Charlock spent a lot of time with his son Ringold, who he sired when he was over eleven years of age. They used to be often seen mooching about the paddock together. Throughout his life Whisky was lucky if he saw eight to ten bitches a year and, for that reason, he was an extraordinary dog for the progeny he produced, some making records. It was not unusual to get more than a couple of good ones in the same litter, and he brought instant success to many breeders.

As was a fact with many notable sires in the past, Charlock was 'full measure' but all quality, although he could have been shorter in the back for better balance. However, he frequently threw up the better compactness of the sire, Black Tulip, and the glorious head stamp of his dam's sire, Blagreaves Bengamino of Ttiweh. Both his parents had beautiful coats and excelled in superb movement, so transmitting these qualities was hardly a problem to him. Overall he was a genetic cocktail of both Black Tulip and Crumpet and inherited their perfect temperaments.

Whisky was indeed a perfect gentleman and a loving pet all his life. He had the same trait as Black Tulip of putting his 'arms' around your neck when you picked him up, showing such affection. He never picked a fight with any of the other dogs and he had a way of dealing with anybody out of line, by merely turning round and glaring at them until they no longer posed a problem.

It was a very sad day indeed when, while racing across the lawn in his twelfth year, he collapsed and died shortly afterwards. He never ran up a vet bill in his life, and he didn't at the finish.

THE GOLDEN YEARS

The early sixties saw the coming of two prominent breeders destined to provide the dogs who were to be the progenitors of some of the finest Cavalier King Charles Spaniels ever to set foot in the show rings not only of Britain but of countless countries around the world.

As the pioneer breeders had provided the type and firm basis upon which the breed was to develop, so the breeders from the sixties onwards for the next three decades were to be brilliant technicians in refining the breed to greater heights. They were strongly influenced by those pioneer breeders and were to produce in abundance Cavaliers who were so pure in breed type and individual in character and appearance that they can never be imitated or rivalled. Quite frankly I was proud to be there to witness it – and hope I can be included in it all.

The past years have certainly seen some beautiful individual dogs, but never quite like

A famous and influential litter of Champions (pictured left to right): Ch. Crisdig Charm, Ch. Crisdig Celebration and Ch. Crisdig Candid.

A 1973 Champion: Pamela Turle's Ch. Sunninghill Broomsquire of Waterston.

An historic day in Cavalier history, Crufts 1973. Susan Burgess with the fabulous Crisdig Florida, judge Viv Bennett, and John Evans with the eventual Best in Show winner, Alansmere Aquarius. Both dogs quickly gained their titles.

those in the 'boom years' where so many great Cavaliers were all alive at the same time. I feel it is regrettable that newcomers to the breed today have never seen those Cavaliers from that bygone era and can only guess, from looking at photographs, what they must have looked like in the flesh. More than a few people, including myself, would probably give almost anything to be able to see those great Cavaliers walk back from the past with their famous handlers through the misty halls of time, just to savour them all one more time.

Susan Burgess' Crisdig Cavaliers and Gertrude Biddle's glamorous Ottermouths created a golden gene pool which was to benefit so many powerful kennels in the following decades. The influence from their dogs is such that it is quite likely to extend well into the 21st century. Mrs Burgess has had so many excellent dogs and bitches over the years that it is difficult to pin-point her most influential Cavaliers. They were a real family of dogs and were almost all as good as one another. Her classical bitches have rivalled the calibre of her stud dogs, none more so than her blenheim bitch Ch. Vairire Charmaine of Crisdig, bred by Mrs Burroughes. Similarly Mrs Biddle also had the great fortune in starting with her 'Dog of a lifetime' in the form of the blenheim bitch Ch. Roulette of Temple Hill, bred by Mrs Eccles. But without doubt many great modern kennels will revere Mrs Biddle's blenheim stud dog Ch. Rose Mullion of Ottermouth with eternal affection and gratefulness for the boost he gave to their fortunes.

THE COAKERS: HOMERBRENT AND HOMARANNE

The best known beneficiary of these two kennels was, of course, the Homerbrent kennel of Molly Coaker and daughter Anne with her Homarannes. Just their one stud dog, Ch. Homaranne Caption, based on Crisdig and Ottermouth lines, brought instant success to many other breeders and put their prefixes 'on the map'. The most notable ones were Gordon and Norma Inglis's early Craigowl Cavaliers, Messrs Rix and Berry's Ricksburys and Mr and Mrs Roy Stevens's Milkeyn dogs.

At their best, the Coaker family's Cavaliers are easily distinguishable by their superb breed type and glamour, coat and nose pigment, but it has been the heads on many of their dogs which have been the signpost of their kennel. As many of the Homerbrent relatives step into the show ring they are easily recognisable by their heads and breed type, and it is quite easy to say "That's a Homerbrent!"

Anne Coaker-Reddaway with (left to right): Ch. Homaranne Caption, Ch. Homaranne Andy Capp, and their dam, Ch. Homerbrent Captivation.

Ch. Craigowl Silkience, owned by Norma Inglis.

The Cavalier King Charles Club Show 1990: Virginia Barwell with Charlottetown Doris Day (Bitch CC), Dog judge Peter Watkins, Bitch judge Joyce Green, and Ken Town's Ch. Barsac The Palio (Dog CC and BIS), who won this event again in 1991.

ALAN HALL AND JOHN EVANS: ALANSMERE

Crisdig and Ottermouth provided many successful combinations in the pedigrees of many notable Cavalier King Charles Spaniels. None more so that the Alansmeres of Alan Hall and John Evans. Their dogs at their best are typical, glamorous and sound, with their large eyes and lovely coats, and always impeccably turned out. The glamorous Rose Mullion bitch, Ch. Bredonvale Mirabelle proved an important acquisition to their kennel, providing them with many lovely dogs over the years, amongst them the lovely blenheim bitches Ch. Alansmere Scarlet O'Hara and Ch. Alansmere Michelle, fondly known as Amice, after the great Mrs Pitt. But it was their three champions Alansmere McGoogans Maggie May, Alansmere Aquarius and Spring Tide of Alansmere who will go down in history.

THE THORNHILLS: KINDRUM

The Thornhill family began their world-famous Kindrum kennel based largely on Pargeter lines; but by introducing outcrosses based on Crisdig and Ottermouth bloodlines, they came to produce a bevy of Cavaliers, truly recognisable as a distinct type, excelling in lovely heads, size and conformation, with profuse silky coats. Their blenheims at their best had brilliant depth of colour. This is another 'family' of Cavaliers who will not forget the dogs that brought them fame, amongst them their great little stud dog Roulette, by Rose Mullion, behind their bloodlines, which later produced the Kindrum's great ambassador in the big rings, in the feminine and vivacious shape of Ch. Kindrum Sylvia and, perhaps, their greatest dual-purpose star, Ch. Alberto of Kindrum, who won several Top Stud dog awards in the early 1990s.

Ch. Alberto of Kindrum (28.8.1986): Toy Group winner and influential stud dog.

Diane Fry, with one of the many Amantra Champions, Ch. Naval Rating of Amantra, judged by Harry Jordan.

THE FRYS: AMANTRA

Diane Fry and daughter Tracy, with the prefix Amantra, will remember their blenheim bitch Alansmere Fiona Harvey with great affection, bred by Messrs Hall and Evans, who started them on a great run of success with three champion children and was grand dam to many more. The Frys early visits to the Coaker family's Ch. Homaranne Andy Capp, plus breeding based predominantly on the great combination of Crisdig and Ottermouth bloodlines, have produced for them ten British champions to date. They have now turned their main attentions to other Toy breeds, gaining great fame in the King Charles Spaniel and Japanese Chin show rings, although the Frys still make an appearance with a nice Cavalier now and again.

MY OWN SALADORS

In the late seventies I was initiated into the Cavalier King Charles Spaniel show and breeding world in no uncertain terms with my first really good Cavalier show bitch, Ch. Salador Crystal Gayle – dropped in at the deep end, during the years when a truly great collection of blenheim bitches were competing for top honours. Arguably so many quality ones of great breed type have never been seen since, at least not all together and at the same time, as they were. There was Messrs Hall and Evans glamour girl, Ch. Alansmere Michelle, and her sister, Gertrude Biddle's Alansmere Minette of Ottermouth, joined later by their younger sister, Bruce Field's pretty bitch, Ch. Alansmere Rosetta of Crieda. Also being shown at the same time was the Thornhills' gorgeous Ch. Kindrum Arabella and Mary Millican Park's outstandingly lovely Ch. Peatland Flora Jensen – possibly, together with Molly Coaker's later Ch. Homerbrent Bewitched, the best of Ch. Homaranne Caption's many champion daughters. This bevy of beauties all around together and mostly turning up in the same classes! I often look back now and wonder if the others used to arrive on the show ground as I did, only to read the catalogue – and groan!

Like those other main kennels, my Salador Cavaliers, whose original bitch Pantisa Christmas Carol went back through Sheila Halsall's Pantisas in direct female line to Ch.

Top Bitch 1992:
Sheila Smith's
Ch. Salador
Celtic Rune.

T. Morgan.,

Vairire Charmaine of Crisdig, were to benefit from Crisdig and Ottermouth bloodlines in due course. The Rose Mullion sons Ch. Bredonvale Bernard and Ronnoc True Luck proved to be great stud dogs for the Salador kennel. Not forgetting, in the early days, Mr and Mrs David Williams' blenheim dog, Ch. Huntsbank Solitaire, alias just William, who played his part in the pedigrees too. Being a singleton, Ch. Huntsbank Solitaire was royally bred by Joyce Green's Ch. Heatherside Fortune out of Ch. Crisdig Rapture, and he became grandsire to champion sister and brother Crystal Gayle and Celtic Prince, top of their sexes in 1979 and 1982.

BREEDING IN THE 1990s
Today in the 1990s in Britain the great 'families' of Cavaliers seem to be disappearing rather too quickly and the breed's future success and development has to rely on the small owners and breeders who produce the single outstanding individual. So, by this token, it is impossible to mention so many individual kennels by name and my apologies to them all. Suffice to say all present-day successful show dogs belong to the discerning breeders and

owners who didn't take very long to recognise what was best in Cavalier King Charles Spaniels from the immediate past and who have continued on in this rich vein.

Elegance with substance: The
1992 Champion, Jenny Hall's Ch.
Muffity Adorable Victoria.

Chapter Seven

THE CAVALIER IN NORTH AMERICA

If ever a breed can truly wear the label "Made in Britain" then it is the Cavalier King Charles Spaniel, but if that famous American gentleman Roswell Eldridge had not journeyed to the UK to place his legendary advertisement in the Crufts catalogue of 1926 to revive the 'Old Type Spaniels', then the canine history books would have possibly been written in quite a different way!

Discerning British breeders and owners are ever-mindful of the gratitude they owe to Roswell Eldridge and the pioneer breeders and, for that reason, right from the beginning, strong and unbreakable associations have existed between the USA and the UK as regards the Cavalier King Charles Spaniel.

THE EARLY HISTORY

Since those early years, when Mr. Eldridge made his solitary and historic crusade to England in search of a breeding pair of the genuine Royal Stuart type spaniels, and his dreams eventually became reality, the great Atlantic ocean has been traversed many times by Cavalier King Charles Spaniel enthusiasts from all walks of life.

While the first Cavalier Champion was made up in Britain in 1948, the first recorded accounts of the arrival of the breed in the USA stem from around 1952. In that year Mrs W. L. Lyons Brown, founder and first president of the Cavalier King Charles Spaniel Club USA, imported her first Cavalier from her good friend Lady Mary Forwood, who bred the famous Eyeworth Cavaliers in England. Two other early imports from England were Mrs John Schiff's Bertie of Rookerynook and Mrs Harold Whitman's English Ch. Jupiter of Ttiweh, bred by Mrs Amice Pitt. Bertie was reputed to have caused quite a stir in his only appearance at an American Kennel Club show, being exhibited in the Miscellaneous class because he was the 'odd man out' amongst the English Toy Spaniels!

But it was Mrs W. L. Lyons Brown's dream to achieve recognition for the breed and she instigated the formation of the Breed Club in 1956 with the aim of attracting all Cavalier fanciers and new owners to arranged get-togethers. A Breed Stud Book was begun then and has been religiously kept up-to-date ever since, recording all American-bred litters. The CKCSC-USA now maintains the Stud Book, together with importation details of Cavaliers arriving from around the world, and organises many Specialty shows confined to the breed all around the country.

RIGHT: Mrs Harold Whitman's Ch. Jupiter of Ttiweh (born 24.8.1949), bred by Amice Pitt, one of the first Cavaliers to arrive from England.

BELOW: A winning progeny class, pictured in the late 1980s. Left to right: UK judge Mary Millicent-Park, Chris Meager, Robbi Jones, Brigida Reynolds with the stud dog Ch. Salador Celtic Dirk, Bill Sloan, Martha Guimond, and UK judge Patricia Thirkell.

Six years after the formation of the new Club in 1956 the first Specialty show was staged at Sutherland in Prospect, Kentucky and was judged by the noted authority, Colonel Joseph C. Quirk, who appraised some forty-three Cavaliers. There were one hundred and eighteen dogs registered by then and the majority, sixty-eight of them, had been bred and raised in the USA from twenty-four litters.

In 1985 the CKCSC-USA celebrated its Silver Jubilee in Prospect, Kentucky, being its twenty-fifth consecutive Specialty show.

On January 10, 1995 the Cavalier King Charles Spaniel was granted American Kennel Club recognition. The registration system was open from March 1st 1995, and breeders and owners are scheduled to exhibit at AKC shows from January 1st 1996. The Registry will remain open for three years. The existing CKCS Club USA was invited by the AKC to be the 'Parent Club', but they declined the invitation.

The result of this has been that a nucleus of experienced breeders, not wishing to see a new club controlled by people who were not fully conversant with the breed, took the initiative and formed their own club, now known as the American Cavalier King Charles Spaniel Club. They applied for Parent Club recognition, and this has been granted.

The Breed Standard will be written and approved by the AKC, with several minor additions for more descriptive purposes, otherwise the Breed Standard will remain virtually the same. The AKC has fulfilled their declared intention, and for the first time since 1960, Cavaliers will no longer be a 'Miscellaneous' breed at AKC shows.

The breed has come a long way in terms of population, as from those first few dogs the USA, together with Australia, are now second in line to the largest populated country, Great Britain, with in excess of 17,000 Cavaliers, most dogs being homebred.

THE JUDGING SYSTEM

Today in the USA Cavalier King Charles Spaniel enthusiasts can avail themselves of approximately twenty-five Breed Specialty shows a year around the country, overseen by the CKCSC-USA. The 'Back-to-Back' two shows a weekend are rather popular, as breeders and owners can gain several objective evaluations about the Cavaliers from experienced, knowledgeable judges, and interested spectators can see as many as two hundred Cavaliers in one day, from young puppies to mature Champions and adults.

The actual judging of the entry by the elected judge is not dissimilar to the UK and other countries, except that the names of the major awards are different and a Championship Points System is employed. After examining each exhibit on a table and watching the dog's movement around and up and down the ring at the trot, the judge places the dogs in merit order in each class, the males being judged separately from the females, except sometimes for mixed classes of Veterans or Braces of dogs.

All unbeaten first prize winners in dogs and bitches go forward as separate sexes to the Final judging, where the Best from all those winners is awarded Winners Dog or, in the case of the females, Winners Bitch. The runner-up to the supreme specimen is awarded Reserve Winners Dog or Bitch. Best in Show is won by either the best dog or the best bitch, and Reserve Best in Show is won by either the runner-up to the same sex as the winner, or by the best of the opposite sex. Best Puppy in Show can be either sex judged the best of all the puppies.

Written critiques are usually given by the judge for publication and can be on as many as four to five places in each class, providing the same dog was unjudged in a previous class. In the UK the major awards are termed Challenge Certificates and Reserve Challenge Certificates, with Best of Breed going to the supreme dog or bitch and Best Opposite Sex or Reserve Best of Breed, depending on the sexes chosen, going to the second best Cavalier. Written critiques are only given on the First and Second places. A Cavalier becomes a Champion after being awarded three Challenge Certificates by three different judges, whether he or she won Best of Breed or not.

Geoffrey Porter (Ireland) judging Elaine Lessig's Ch. Salador Catrina of Roi L.

THE CHAMPIONSHIP POINT SYSTEM

At CKCSC-USA or CKCSC Regional Championship shows held under CKCSC-USA Regulations, points will be awarded as follows:

BEST IN SHOW (BIS): One point more than the highest number of points available to either sex based on the Major points from the Scale of Points below.

RESERVE BEST IN SHOW (RBIS): One point less than Best in Show.

WINNERS DOG & BITCH (WD & WB): Highest number of points available in sex based on the Major Points from the Scale of Points below.

RESERVE WINNERS DOG OR BITCH (RWD & RWB): One point less than Winners Dog or Winners Bitch.

BEST PUPPY IN SHOW (BPIS): Highest number of points available from the Junior and Senior Puppy classes based on the Class Points from the Scale of Points below. (If the entry justifies and points are awarded in any of the Puppy classes, Best Puppy would be awarded the 1 or 2 Class Points even if the class had less than four (4) entries.) At any given show, the dogs chosen BIS and RBIS shall only retain the points for that win.

SCALE OF POINTS

MAJOR POINTS

Dogs in Competition	Bitches in Competition	Points
12-20	12-20	3
21-30	21-30	4
31-40	31-40	5
41-50	41-50	6
51 or more	51 or more	7

CLASS POINTS

Total Dogs and Bitches in Competition	Dogs or Bitches Competing In Class	Points for Class winners
1-39	NA	0
40-59	at least 4	1
60 or more	at least 4	2

Cavaliers winning Major Points will not retain Class Points in that show. No Cavalier may receive Class Points from more than one win at any show.

CHAMPIONSHIP AWARDS

 A dog or bitch must accumulate 10 points at CKCSC-USA or CKCSC Regional Championship shows held under CKCSC regulations. These 10 points must include two Major wins (3 points or better) under two different judges in two different shows, in addition to at least one point under a third judge.

 The Board of Directors is authorised to modify the Scale of Points or number of points needed to qualify for the title of Champion as and if the number of Cavaliers and/or shows changes.

 The organisers of the Specialty shows frequently invite overseas Breed Specialty Judges to officiate at their shows to glean some of the best opinions, many of these being British judges who frequently remark on the wonderful reception and hospitality shown to them on their judging trips to the USA. By the same token, overseas Cavalier breeders and owners, particularly the British, look forward to returning the welcome and bonhomie which exists between the two countries.

 The most popular meeting places are Crufts Dog Show, and the British 'mother' Club's annual show, held in the spring. The cream of British Cavaliers can be seen at these prestigious events and, over the years, American breeders and enthusiasts have gone to a lot of trouble and expense to make the journey in order to look, to compare notes and, frequently, to acquire breeding stock to further their own programmes. Many Cavalier King Charles Spaniels have left these shores bound for the USA, including British Champions and beautiful young dogs – but some, one can say, were so mediocre that they were deported rather than exported. However the US has a multitude of talented breeders who know what they are about and have been quietly getting on with it over the years. Many Cavaliers, after completing their Championship show titles, go on to compete and win Working and Obedience qualifications.

THE BREEDERS

Besides Cavaliers being imported from most parts of the world into the USA, many of the early dogs and the bulk of today's importations come from the UK and Ireland. Dogs chiefly from some of the early prominent kennels were the foundation for most of the individual American strains, none more so than the Cavaliers from the famous Pargeter kennel of Mrs Barbara Keswick, a lady who sent many good dogs to major countries all over the world.

One of her many beneficiaries was, in the early days, a prominent breeder and exhibitor, Miss Elizabeth Spalding with her Kilspindie Cavaliers, who was President of the CKCSC-USA Club from 1968 to 1972, succeeding Mrs George Garvin Brown, and again from 1987 to 1989.

During the last twenty years one can state quite safely, without fear of contradiction, that the USA has benefited immeasurably from at least one British kennel based firmly, again, on Pargeter bloodlines – Mrs Pam Thornhill's outstanding Kindrum dogs. This can be said without detracting from the many other dogs from most of the prominent modern-day British kennels which can be found in the US; and, as has been discussed in this book, most of them usually stem from the same golden gene pool and family tree and, for that reason, have the happy knack of blending together and complementing one another.

Even if the British 'boom' years' influence arrived a little late in the USA, the Breed type, quality and Standard of the Cavalier King Charles Spaniel show dogs have risen to such heights that one can now honestly say that they can compete with dogs anywhere in the world – and one can now sincerely add the words left off – and win! Indeed I can see the day when American dogs will be imported back into Britain, to breed back in the qualities which I feel the Brits have been very complacent and remiss about, one quality being the huge, dark eyes, which are fast disappearing in British dogs.

Limits of space prevent mention of all the Cavalier King Charles Spaniel breeders and owners resident in the USA and Canada who have, with their dogs, contributed towards the high standard and steady development of the breed, but one would be very remiss if mention is not made of the following breeders, in alphabetical order, who have made more than a significant contribution.

JO ANN CARVILL: BJ CAVALIERS

Where better to start than with Jo Ann Carvill and her BJ Cavaliers. Besides being the breeder of many lovely dogs, she is the proud owner and breeder of Ch. BJ Holy Terror, a blenheim dog who is the undisputed Top Winning Cavalier of all time in the US with a string of top winners, and who is still being exhibited. Suffice it to say, many of his top wins are awarded by visiting Breed Specialists and, with Champion offspring, he has not disappointed as a stud dog either. He is truly a dog who can compete and win anywhere in the world.

Pam Rooney (UK) judging Jo-Ann Carvill's Ch. BJ Holy Terror, the top winning Cavalier of all time in the USA

Ch. B.J. Holy Terror's daughter, Ch. B.J. Here We Go Again, with Elaine Lessing and Colin Fereday (UK) judging.

GAMMON AND SCHROLL: RAVENRUSH

Messrs Gammon and Schroll have bred and campaigned many typical and quality dogs under their Ravenrush affix, amongst them the big-winning ruby dog Ch. Kindrum Redcoat of Ravenrush, bred by Pam Thornhill, the dual-purpose blenheim dog Ch. Ravenrush Tartan, and Paula Campanozzi's Ch. Ravenrush Best Dressed, a beautiful-headed tricolour male of true breed type.

BARBARA GARNETT SMITH: LAUGHING CAVALIERS

Barbara Garnett Smith, with her Laughing Cavaliers has spared no expense in purchasing and importing English dogs, and she was fortunate in acquiring, amongst others, the blenheim dog Eng. Ch. Alansmere Rhett Butler and the Crufts CC winning blenheim bitch Eng. Ch. Sukev Dolly Daydream, imported in whelp to Eng. Ch. Salador Crismark, besides good stock from the Fry's Amantra Kennel.

The lovely head and breed type displayed by Paula Campanozzi's Ch. Ravenrush Best Dressed.

CANADIAN CONNECTIONS

Chris Gingell, resident in Canada, deserves a mention with her Caruaidd Cavaliers, and she is also a Director on the board of the CKCS Club of Canada. Martha Guimond's Top tricolour Stud dog 1992, Ch. & Can. Ch. Rutherford Elliot of Shagbark, has strong connections with Canada, being sired by Mrs Brigida Reynold's tricolour Ch. Salador Celtic Dirk, who won a similar accolade. Elliot was bred by Robbi Jones and has stood out for the quality and numbers of his top progeny.

ROBBI JONES: RUTHERFORD CAVALIERS

Robbi Jones, with her Rutherford Cavaliers, has been a clever and astute breeder, with fortunate purchases from Pam Thornhill's Kindrum kennel. Her blenheim stud Ch. Kindrum Lucifer preceded his son Elliot by winning the Top Stud Dog award in 1991. Amongst his many winning progeny is Top Cavalier Ch. BJ Holy Terror. The blenheim bitch Ch. Kindrum Alice at Rutherford, Top Brood Bitch in 1990, is typical of the dual-purpose stock she represents – they win and breed winners.

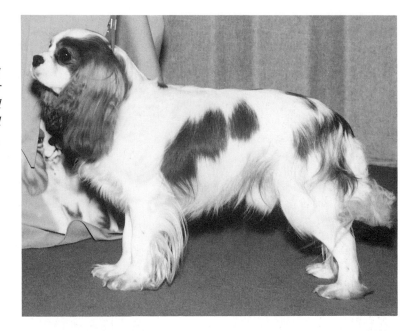

Influential stud dog Ch. Kindrum Lucifer of Rutherford, bred by Pam Thornhill (UK).

Martha Guimond's influential stud dog, Ch. Rutherford Elliot of Shagbark.

The beautiful head and breed type of multi Ch. Rocky Raccoon of Wyndcrest, aged ten years. Owned by Mr and Mrs Harold Letterly.

A GREAT CHAMPION

I don't think there can be a true Cavalier show enthusiast in the world who has not heard of the Cavalier CKCSC-US, Can. Mex. Americas and World Ch. Rocky Raccoon of Wyndcrest, owned by Harold and Joan Letterly and bred by Olive Derbyshire. A blenheim male bred from Amantra and Kindrum bloodlines, he became a legend in his own lifetime by virtue of his illustrious show career and achievements as a stud dog but is now sadly deceased. I was fortunate, while holidaying in Arizona a few years ago, to make his acquaintance, and it wasn't difficult to see from where his best progeny had inherited the great breed type and really lovely, glamorous heads with the much sought-after huge, dark eyes.

BRIGIDA REYNOLD: MOSTYN CAVALIERS

Also resident in Canada are Mrs Brigida Reynold's Mostyn Cavaliers. She has produced many lovely dogs based on similar bloodlines to the other progressive breeders, but she reveres her great stud dog Ch. Salador Celtic Dirk, tricolour son of English Champions Celtic Prince and Colleen, as the one who became a bit of a legend, especially in the USA.

ANN ROBINS: CHADWICK CAVALIERS

In her early days Ann Robins of the Chadwick Cavaliers promoted dogs from the famous English Maxholt kennel of Mrs Talbot and she is a breeder who makes frequent trips to England to further her bloodlines.

THAEDER: REDTHEA CAVALIERS

If the old adage is true that "the strength of a kennel lies in its bitches", then the Thaeders'

Karin Ostmann's Ch.
Sheeba Special
Edition: Best in Show
at the CNE 1995.

Redthea Cavaliers have everything to look forward to in the future, judging by the beautiful stock they have already produced.

SUMMARY

One cannot end this chapter without thinking about Roswell Eldridge all those years ago – what would he have wanted for the breed he strove to revive? Perhaps the answer lies in the fact that he placed his historical advertisement in neither a newspaper nor in a magazine. He displayed it in full view of serious, dedicated breeders at an official Kennel Club show – and one which oversaw all the country's relevant Breed Clubs.

Chapter Eight

THE INTERNATIONAL SCENE

Cavalier King Charles Spaniels from just about every modern British blood line have found their way around the world.

EUROPE
The first person to import a Cavalier into Europe was Mme Van der Boom, who acquired the famous blenheim stud and show dog Swed. Ch. Kingmaker of Ttiweh from Amice Pitt. Since then there have been many imports and, subsequently, numerous successful kennels have emerged. One prominent breeder deserving mention is the Netherlands-based kennel of Mr Hans Boelaars, whose Lamslag affix has been synonymous with outstanding type and quality for many years.

Swed. Ch. Kingmaker of Ttiweh: An early import into Europe.

Madame Van der Boom and her Cavaliers.

Judge Pam Thornhill with her Best Breeding Group in Sweden in 1992, the Rodero's kennel, owned by Laila Lansberg Larsson.

For some reason, very few breeders from Germany are registered with the English Cavalier King Charles Spaniel Club; perhaps the breed is in such totally soft contrast to the country's traditionally hard-as-nails 'Dogs of War', such as the Doberman, German Shepherd and Rotweiller.

SCANDINAVIA

Sweden and Finland have to be two of the breed's most populated countries, where one finds Cavaliers of outstanding soundness, because they enjoy particularly stringent Kennel Club control, designed to promote their welfare and development. The system there certainly sorts the men out from the boys as regards the judges, who have to provide an instant grading, signified by a coloured ribbon tied to the dog's lead, and a critique given on each dog, there and then in the ring, with no time to go home and think about it. One has to know what one is about and to be word perfect. A fake can be spotted straight-away by the ringside spectators! By the same token, a judge is instructed by the authorities to banish any incompetent steward from the ring, who is immediately replaced with another.

My recent memories of Sweden include judging a memorable Breeders Group class headed by the Sperringgarden kennel, who have enjoyed much success for a long time. In Finland I judged some of the prettiest Cavaliers in a huge representative entry, with really excellent colours in all four varieties.

AUSTRALIA AND NEW ZEALAND

As the USA has been the undisputed beneficiary of such kennels as Pam Thornhill's Kindrum Cavaliers, so Australia and New Zealand have almost made the Homerbrent and

Jenny Egan and Aust. NZ Ch.
Homerbrent Cartoon.

Homaranne Cavaliers of the Coaker family a religion! Early imports included Betty Reading's Eng. Ch. Pargeter Trillium of Ttiweh, carrying both affixes of Barbara Keswick and Amice Pitt, and, later, Caption's sire, Aust. Ch. Homerbrent Henry, both notable blenheim stud dogs.

Margaret Franze, greatly assisted by husband Ralph, did much to promote the breed in the early days. They even showed their team of Le Chevalier Champions against one another, in order to promote more competition and Breed class guarantee, with a view to eventually achieving Group status. Their early imports included the Frys' tricolour dog, Eng. Ch. Amantra Bohemian Rhapsody, who enjoyed many top wins; but Le Chevalier revere their first import as their best, Eng. Ch. Crisdig Leading Seaman's blenheim son, Aust. Ch. Able Seaman of Amantra, who sired eighteen Champions for the home kennel.

Australia's top winning Cavalier of all time is Aust. & NZ Ch. Homerbrent Cartoon, a blenheim male bred by Molly Coaker and owned in partnership with Mr and Mrs Egan and Mr and Mrs Murdoch.

IRELAND

Ireland is truly a very green and mystical land and it is very hard to come home from there! The Irish hospitality is just about as legendary as the thoroughbreds raised in the country – as, indeed, are the Cavalier King Charles Spaniels.

One kennel affix synonymous with Ireland has been that of Mrs E. J. Nugent with her Tnegun Cavaliers, who have enjoyed much success, with many Champions registered on both sides of the Irish Sea at the English and Irish Kennel Clubs. Mrs Nugent must have the unique distinction of being the breeder who has judged and bred the Best in Show winning dog at the St Patrick's Day All Breed Championship Dog Show, Ireland's equivalent to England's prestigious Crufts Dog Show. Her blenheim dog Tnegun Return Train, owned by the late Colin Foster, was the first Cavalier to record this win. He had also won two English CCs when he was tragically run over and killed in Dublin.

Mr and Mrs Robert Lamont's blenheim dog, Irish Ch. Caerwen Cachemire of Moorfields, bred by England's Ann Cartwright, repeated the win many years later, and has won several Top Stud dog awards. But without doubt one of the most prepotent blenheim stud dogs to dominate the Irish and English show scene in recent years has been Rose Mullion's

Heather Lamont with her Irish Champions and CC winners Caerwen Chanelle of Moorfields and Caerwen Cachemire of Moorfields.

Int. Ch. Sunninghill Perseus of Lochefee and Irish Ch. Ben Gorm of Lochfee.

*Irish Ch.
Tnegun Return
Train: Winner
of two CCs.*

*Ronnoc True
Luck's 'All
Champion' litter to
Salador Country
Girl (second left):
Ch. Salador
Connors, Ch.
Salador Corrigan
and Ch. Salador
Colleen.*

blenheim son, Ronnoc True Luck. His story must stand as exemplary evidence of his owner's early faith in him and so give encouragement to other breeders who are given the same unwelcome and, perhaps, uninvited advice by an independent party!

When True Luck's owners, Paddy and Gerard Connor, took him to his first and only dog show the judge told them to take the dog home and forget about him. This opinion might have been arrived at because of True Luck's mismarked face, with the brown tan extending down to his nose on one side. Fortunately for the history of the breed, the Connor brothers kept him. Lucky was one of a very large litter of puppies, bred by Mr Richardson out of the CC winning bitch Kerkhove Frolicsome by Ch. Rose Mullion of Ottermouth, and the last to go. He was a sterling example of the prepotency generated by mixing Crisdig and Ottermouth breeding together.

The Connor brothers were fortunate in the beginning in acquiring three Tnegun bitches from Mrs Nugent, who had started with similar lines to Susan Burgess and Gertrude Biddle and, like them, had a foundation Champion bitch who assured her early good fortune. She was a blenheim bitch, Int. Ch. Clohamon Heatherbell of Lochfee. The latter affix belonged to another Irish stalwart, Mrs Bartels, who owned, in partnership with Miss Turle, the famous blenheim stud and show dog Int. Ch. Sunninghill Perseus of Lochfee.

When I was judging Cavaliers in Ireland in the early eighties, the progeny of one dog seemed continually to impress and to dominate the Class winners and Best of Breed. They were all sired by Ronnoc True Luck and so, when I returned to England, I looked on it as an omen when the first bitch to come in season was the dual CC and Toy Group winner, Country Girl, Crismark's sister. There was this matter of urgency, due to the fact that Ronnoc True Luck was, I found to my delight, still alive, but very old. However, he did sire my record All Champion litter, numbering three puppies, when he was over twelve years of age. This proved to be his last but one litter. If ever a dog lived up to his name then Ronnoc True Luck surely did.

The Connor brothers' generosity in allowing such an elderly dog to be used accompanied their game suggestion to 'swop a stud' so no money changed hands – a rare attitude that could be adopted by many modern-day stud dog owners to advantage. Their generosity was much appreciated and will never be forgotten.

Despite the many years of trouble in Ireland, which thankfully looks like coming to an end, the route to Castleblayney has taken on a certain air of pilgrimage for the many overseas and British breeders who visit the famous Ronnoc kennel.

Perhaps due to the troubles, many gorgeous puppies have never realised their full potential and have been sold away into pet homes. But the ones who have found their way into discerning breeders' hands have made their mark, and other British kennels to benefit highly have been those of Amantra, Cottismeer, Homerbrent, and the modern-day kennel enjoying much success based on Ronnoc bloodlines, the Fox's Pamedna kennel.

Chapter Nine

WHOLE COLOURS

From the beginning whole colours have played an important role in the make-up of outstanding particolours. Right there at the start was Cannonhill Richey, the ruby sire of Ch. Daywell Roger. Whole colours continued to appear regularly in the particolour pedigrees right down to the 'boom' years in the sixties and seventies. Two important examples during that era, which immediately spring to mind, are Vairire Isis, the ruby dam of the important stud dog Ch. Vairire Osiris, and the black and tan Rhea of Eyeworth, daughter of Lady Mary Forwood's beloved Venus of Eyeworth, and the dam of Ch. Roulette of Temple Hill. To say their lines went on to great things would be rather an understatement.

THE POOR RELATIONS
Whole colours were often referred to as the 'poor relations', never really enjoying the exposure and the winning ways of the tricolours and blenheims, yet there they were, making their contribution to the breed. In all honesty, the whole colours did look different to the partis and they rarely appealed to the judges. Because of this not many owners and breeders showed much interest in keeping them, knowing that it was an uphill struggle to find interested customers for any puppies they bred, or any gratification in the show ring. Due to their glamour and greater appeal in appearance to the breeder, the judge and the pet owner, the particolours made greater strides. There were some lovely heads, glamorous coats and much more opportunity and choice when it came to breeding out the constructional faults.

This phenomenon was reflected in the fact that, from 1948 to the appearance of Ch. Caderyn Black Tulip in 1977, almost thirty years later, there had only been nineteen Champion whole colours as opposed to one hundred and ninety-six particolour title holders.

GROWING INTEREST
Amongst the pedigrees of those nineteen wholecolour Champions were, of course, Amice Pitt's Ttiwehs, coming from Mrs Jennings' Plantations, who were also behind Mrs Rennie's black and tan dog, Ch. Royalist of Veren. Royalist became grandsire to Mrs Patten's black and tan bitch Ch. Barings Elizabertha, reputed to be a lovely bitch, followed a few years later by another of Mrs Patten's, the big winning black and tan bitch, Ch. Barings Claramara, bred by Mrs Preece. Her Chandlers prefix was to become a household name wherever whole colours were discussed. Also in the fifties, Lady Forwood, who was to

Judy Watts Davies' Ch. Caderyn Black Tulip.

enjoy success with all four colours, made up another Royalist grandchild in the black and tan dog, Ch. Cointreau of Eyeworth. Mrs Patten was to make it a triple ace when she bred Claramara's black and tan daughter, Barings Margareta, who was owned by, and carried the well-known prefix, Millstone, of Evelyn Booth. She was another member of an elite group of breeders, which also included Diane Schilizzi's Chacombes and Sheila Halsall's Pantisas, who were to make up or breed English champions in three different colours; and this was probably the key to where the gradual, progressive improvement and success of the whole colours lay – having the interest and the 'eye' of those breeders who encompassed all the four colours in their endeavours.

In 1988, forty years on from Ch. Daywell Roger, the Saladors, bred or owned by me, were to become the first kennel to complete the unique record of the four different coloured Champions, although the fourth coloured dog, not technically bred by the kennel like the other three, was rich with Salador blood.

In 1994 the Miltons' Fontelanias completed the record of all four different coloured Champions being bred and owned by them.

In her wholecolour Champions, Diane Schilizzi was to promote the breeding of that single-minded supporter of the colours, Molly Marshall of the Kormars, while other breeders, frustrated and still dissatisfied with the looks and limitations of the whole colours and their pedigrees, were not afraid to lean towards the particolours for some help. After all, the whole colours had been waiting far too long in the wings, they had played an important roll in the particolour pedigrees of yesteryears, and it was time for them to start taking centre stage.

This progressive move on the part of those breeders was to be, in actual fact, blessed by the great Amice Pitt. While she and Evelyn Booth were sitting at the side of the ring after the latter had completed her judging at the Club show in 1967, Evelyn Booth complained

Geoffrey Porter's Int. Ch. Kindrum Rose Red.

that the whole colours on the whole were very disappointing. Amice Pitt's forthright reply came: "So they will be until breeders bring in some good blenheim or tricolour blood."

What were those breeders after and what were their aims, so that they could produce dogs who could compete on equal terms with the high standard of blenheims and tricolours? It was better heads, balanced classical outlines with the correct angled fore and hindquarters and those glamorous straight, silky coats so enjoyed by the partis. Added to which, they had to capture that elusive, charismatic breed type and quality which would make the judge look at them twice. Most of all, because the whole colours were plain anyway in appearance compared with the flashiness of the partis, the two most important qualities would have to be outstanding movement and show temperament. Then they would stand out in a crowd.

One such breeder with a flair for whole colours was Pam Thornhill of Cambridge who bred, amongst others, Gammon and Schroll's Ch. Kindrum Redcoat of Ravenrush, a big winner in the USA. Geoffrey Porter's Int. Ch. Kindrum Rose Red is still, at the time of writing, the only wholecolour champion on both sides of the Irish Sea. Both these rubies had a blenheim parent.

After outcrossing to particolour lines, it is interesting to note how many whole colours in the breed's history, after pinching the desired breed qualities of the partis, in a generation or two revert to becoming wholecolour dominant. Breeders are always worried about mis-marking when mixing colours, but in fact a dominant wholecolour – that is to say, a dog which only produces its own colour whatever colour it is mated to – often produces whole colours with no white hairs on the puppies at all.

When I became interested in the breed in the late seventies, the wholecolour sire who was much talked about was Rhosnesney Prince Ivan of Rhybank – an unlucky black and tan dog, perhaps, because after two CCs and seven Reserve CCs his title eluded him, although he was one of the few to gain a Junior Warrant in those days. Ivan was bred by the late West Country breeder Mary Parkinson, who also sold to other ownership the CC winners Arkle and Black Knight. Heather Fereday remembered the day well when she bought Ivan as a puppy from Miss Parkinson for £25. The two ladies met outside Bristol Zoo and Ivan yapped all the way home in the back of the car!

CH. CADERYN BLACK TULIP AND FAMILY

While watching a televised production of *David Copperfield* one Sunday afternoon my eyes became riveted by the dog sitting on the settee in one of the scenes. It was a black and tan Cavalier King Charles Spaniel and this was to be the start of a life-long love affair with the colour, and I just had to have one. By coincidence, the next weekend was the Wellington Christmas dog show in Shropshire, which was packed out with people and dogs. It was unbearably hot and the only empty spaces were the small judging rings – but across the crowded room my eyes met those of a dark, handsome stranger!

No, it wasn't a man but a black and tan Cavalier, sitting in the lap of a very flushed-faced lady wearing a woolly hat. This was my first encounter with Judy Watts from Hereford and her then virtually unknown Caderyn Black Tulip. I couldn't take my eyes off this dog, for he had a magical aura about him. So, very apprehensive because my only breedable bitch was a tricolour and the lady was quite likely to refuse me, I decided to ask her if I could use him at stud. Well, she didn't say yes or no at the time, but when I rang her at home when Salador Crumpet came in season, she said 'yes', and seven puppies resulted, all the four colours and individually well-marked.

More delight followed when my 'find', Black Tulip, gained his title during the following show season, as did his younger brother Ch. Niccoli of Rhybank, owned by Heather Fereday, who also had the sire, Ivan. Both brothers went on to sire Champion progeny. Black Tulip's ruby daughter, Mrs Martin's Ch. Wolvershill Hannah, had the distinction of winning the bitch CC two years running at the Club show.

Ch. Caderyn Black Tulip captured the imagination of many people besides myself. What made him special was his glorious and natural high head carriage and floating, ground-covering gait. His beautiful eyes, profuse silky coat, lovely size, make and shape all added to his charm. Above all he had the most impeccable temperament and, when you picked 'Sammy' up, he was so affectionate, actually putting his paws around your neck and snuggling into your face and neck. This trait was to be passed down through what was, eventually, to prove to be a great male line. These days people often tell me about their own black and tans doing this very thing – well, that's where it came from. More important, such was the influence from this pedigree that, today, the descendants can be easily spotted across

Sheila Smith's Salador Crumpet and Salador Cherrybird.   *Photo: Anne Roslin-Williams.*

the show ring by their distinctive breed type and characteristic movement. Black Tulip, and his parents Ivan and Laughernbrook April Love, lived well into their teens, which was another good reason for using the bloodlines.

April Love was sired by Millstone Eustace, the direct result of that inspirational ringside conversation between his breeder, Evelyn Booth, and Amice Pitt, being a union between Mrs Preece's black and tan Chandlers Phalaris and Evelyn's tricolour Millstone Henrietta. Eustace also sired, amongst others, Evelyn's special pride and joy, Ch. Millstone Beechking Tansy, a black and tan bitch with much particolour influence in the pedigree.

Ch. Niccoli of Rhybank gave Jo Blunt, from Northampton, Ch. Karabel Caprice and Corinthian, the latter being the sire of Mr and Mrs Hugh Inman's foundation bitch for their wholecolour line. Black Tulip gave me the well-marked black and tan Salador Charlock and his beautifully marked blenheim sister with the lozenge, Salador Cherrybird, from their tricolour dam Crumpet. There lay another prophetic coincidence from that ringside conversation, because Crumpet was sired by Barbara Palfree's gorgeous-headed tricolour Blagreaves Bengamino of Ttiweh, a male heavily linebred to the Ttiwehs.

From here this family branched out into many successful roots for many breeders of all four colours, the whole colours once again playing a big role behind some outstanding particolours. Not only were the whole colours making their presence felt, but they were starting to make records into the bargain.

For my kennel, probably the most outstanding particolour bred was Ch. Salador Celtic Prince from Cherrybird, who had bred, in an earlier litter, his older sister and the first Champion for the kennel, Ch. Salador Crystal Gayle. Although having a black and tan grandfather, Celtic Prince was a perfectly marked tricolour. He still holds the record as the youngest post-war breed champion, at twelve and a half months. His eleven CCs and seven Reserve CCs were awarded by most of the other leading breeders and top all-rounders, which spoke for itself. He went on to sire five British Champions and numerous overseas Champions and CC winners, so his untimely death from a collapsed lung while still in his prime made the loss very hard to come to terms with. A very brave dog, whom everyone tried desperately to save.

JOAN PAGAN'S SORATAS AND DESCENDANTS

No chapter on whole colours would be complete without mentioning Joan Pagan's Essex-based Sorata kennel. Her dogs at their best, excelling in breed type, quality and superb coat and nose pigmentation, have made a tremendous impact on wholecolour showdogs. She really struck gold when she bred the litter containing Llewellyn, Lawrence and Lucilla, grandchildren of Charlock, and with another line to Black Tulip.

Joan Pagan's Sorata Llewellyn.

Lucy Koster's Ch. Knight Magic at Harana.

Lucy Koster's Ch. Harana Rockstar of Denstone.

Photo: T. Morgan.

Sheila Smith's Ch.
Rheinvelt Ringold
v. Salador.

Photo:
Diane Pearce.

*Dr Richard
Gilmour-Smith's
Aust. Ch.
Chamanic
Centaurus.*

*Ch. Rheinvelt
Red Hot, bred
and owned by
Mrs A. and Miss
J. Potter.*

*Photo:
T. Morgan.*

*Mr and Mrs
Hugh Inman's
Ch. Chamanic
Lucasta.*

*Mr and Mrs R.
Dix's Pippbrook
Theobald.*

Sorata Llewellyn sired Ch. Sorata Fissical, an utterly stunning ruby male. He had the capacity for making most other coloured dogs in his class look rather ordinary as soon as he stepped into the ring. His younger brother, Raffles, went to live with Elizabeth Ryan in Ireland, becoming an Irish Champion and winning two English CCs. Ch. Sorata Dunross was another Llewellyn son for the home kennel. Sorata Lawrence sired the black and tans Sorata Linda and Lynette, both notable brood bitches.

From Linda came Lucy Koster's Ch. Knight Magic at Harana, bred by Shirley Appelby, who combined the Downsbank lines of Ruth Mochrie's Stafford-based kennel. Ruth had also fallen under the spell of Black Tulip and used him to great advantage in her early dogs. Fissical and Knight Magic went on to further these highly successful lines with more Champions and CC winners, including dogs from Maureen Milton's Fontelania kennel, Molly Coaker's Homerbrents in South Devon and George and Morag Donaldson's Linvids.

Knight Magic turned out to be some sire, and breeders were still adding to the impressive list of Champions and CC winners long after he was tragically run over and killed while still in his prime. This was a fate shared by one of his Champion sons, the Shepherds' Ch. Saleres Little Richard. These deaths were felt heavily in the Cavalier world by many people.

Andree Potter and daughter Julie were quite convinced that Sorata Lynette was going to click with Celtic Prince and she did, in a way, because she produced the well-known brood bitches, Rheinvelt Celtic Lass and Celtic Dancer, the latter producing Mrs Khan's Marelza Black Knight, when mated back to Knight Magic. Several years later, Celtic Lass came back to visit the elderly but very frisky Charlock. Two black and tan male puppies were born and, as the Potters decided they didn't want to keep boys, I had the great fortune to be offered both of them. One of them, Roberto, became a Champion overseas and the other became Ch. Rheinvelt Ringold v. Salador, who won his first CC at his first general Championship show and his title at sixteen months, the record for a black and tan male. He shares the record number of five CCs with his half-brother, the Miltons' Ch. Fontelania Burnt Toast, who was another great loss of a very promising stud dog, through ill luck at an early age. Like his predecessors, Ringold has not disappointed as a stud dog.

Ringold's son, the Kosters' Ch. Harana Rockstar of Denstone has got off to a great start with his stud career, siring the Potters' Ch. Rheinvelt Red Hot, herself the youngest ruby bitch to gain a title, at eighteen months. The youngest black and tan bitch would have been Mrs Booth's Ch. Millstone Barings Margareta, at twenty-five months.

Hugh and Jocelyn Inman, from Cheshire, were first persuaded by friends to take up the pursuit of dog showing. Their house pet, Starry Trefoil of Chamanic by Karabel Corinthian, proved to be a real gem of a brood bitch, producing six puppies in two litters to Charlock. Amongst these was Dr Richard Gilmour-Smith's Aust. Ch. Chamanic Centaurus, who became the first black and tan to win a Best in Show at an All-breeds Championship show 'down under', and he went on to do it twice more. His brother, Trafalgar, won a CC and the Junior Warrant, whilst his sister, Ch. Chamanic Finistere, won five CCs and looked like beating the record of six CCs set by Amice Pitt's Ch. Amanda Loo of Ttiweh in 1949 until an accident prevented her from continuing a very successful show campaign.

Her ruby daughter Bell Rock, sired by Mo and Arnold Close's CC winning Chandlers Prince Barle and bred by Mrs Preece proved to be another great brood bitch. Mated back to her grandfather Charlock, she bred the siblings Shannon, two CCs and Rosslare, one CC. To Sorata Llewellyn she bred the ruby bitch Ch. Chamanic Lucasta, who did become the record holder of the highest number of CCs – nine, including one won at Crufts. Her sister Leonie, when mated to Ringold several years later, bred Ch. Buckny Mellowman of Chamanic and his CC winning sister, Buckny Ebony.

The third member of that all-important litter bred by Joan Pagan was Sorata Lucilla, owned by Mick and Lil Shinnick from Essex. Their Leelyn kennel has bred some lovely whole colours and their influential ruby stud dog Chagarl has brought them much success. Chagarl and his black and tan brother Black Bruno were sired by Charlock. Chagarl, as is always the way, was used more than his brother and, amongst many CC winners, came Joan's Ch. Sorata Myfanwy and Mr and Mrs Smith's Ch. Jowida Charlotte Rose of Mishana. From Evelyn Booth's Ch. Millstone Beechking Tansy mated to Mrs Seager's Waggoners Whispered Pledge came Millstone Basil. He was to sire a much-loved personality in the Cavalier world, in Britain as well as overseas, in the shape of Pippbrook Theobald, who was a black and tan male, owed by Chris and Rob Dix, who lived to a great old age. Although he was a successful show and stud dog, his main forte and domain became the Veteran classes, where he notched up many wins.

THE CHANGE IN FORTUNES

So, from the early seventies, there came about a complete reversal in the fortunes of the whole colours. Whereas it had been a rare sight to see a wholecolour top a championship show entry, let alone do the Double – that is to win both Challenge Certificates at the same show – now this is no longer the case and the whole colours are a force to be reckoned with at any level of competition, even to being short-listed and placed in the highly competitive Toy Groups. Such is the popularity of the whole colours nowadays that we see breeders and owners, who have not shown a previous active interest in the colours, suddenly acquiring them for breeding, for exhibition and for very eye-catching quality pets.

The top winning force and success of present-day whole colours has been further magnified since the early seventies by Top Stud awards being won by two rubies and two black and tan males, all from the same family.

Ch. Stellers's Eider of Pantisa won the Stud Dog Trophy in 1972 for his owners, Mr and Mrs Duncan Gillies. Bred by Sheila Halsall, he was a ruby grandson of Ch. Cointreau of Eyeworth and German, Dutch and Belgian Ch. Pantisa Redshank of Sunninghill. The pedigree then drops down in direct tail line through Eider's grandson Rhosnesney Prince Ivan of Rhybank, through Ch. Caderyn Black Tulip to Salador Charlock, who won *Dog World* Top Cavalier stud dog in 1986. Similar accolades were awarded to Sorata Llewellyn and Ch. Knight Magic of Harana in due course. It was no mean feat for any of them, considering the great numbers of Cavaliers being bred from in the other colours, creating keen competition.

What a turn-around in the fortunes of the whole colours since those early days! And breeders can continue in this highly successful vein for a long time yet. As wholecolour pedigrees stand at present, generally they are still in a condensed form and do not present such a hotchpotch, as many of the particolour pedigrees do today.

*Mr and Mrs
Duncan Gillies'
Ch. Stellers
Eider of Pantisa.*

*Photo:
Diane Pearce.*

*Sheila Smith's
Ch. Salador
Coppergleam.*

THE FUTURE

For the future, the breeders, in their endeavours, must conserve and consolidate all those qualities which the previous generation bred into the particolours. The main feature, to which special attention must be given, is the head. Deep stops that one can press a thumb into, pronounced foreheads and too short a muzzle are not only incorrect, but very untypical. Take the photograph of Ch. Knight Magic of Harana for example. Paint an imaginary white blaze up the centre of the head and there you have a perfect particolour head.

In 1989, at Crufts, probably the best known dog show in the world, Cavalier King Charles Spaniels were judged by Brigadier Jack Burgess in, sadly, his last judging engagement. He had probably been more associated with blenheims and tricolours, and he had seen the best. The wholecolour devotees also remember it as the day when a unique record was set, never achieved before at this prestigious show. With a star-studded entry, and plenty of choice, the Brigadier made a statement when he awarded both Challenge Certificates to wholecolour Cavaliers, namely Ch. Rheinvelt Ringold v. Salador, Best of Breed, and Ch. Chamanic Lucasta. For those wholecolour enthusiasts watching from the crowd, this event must have set a golden seal on their remarkable development and dominance in the breed today.

Chapter Ten

KEEPING THINGS SIMPLE

In this day and age, with so many technical and diagnostic techniques available to the modern day breeder, people sometimes lose sight of the simple essential rules and traditions that earlier breeders used and, indeed, learned to rely on when it was necessary for their own inborn talent and intuition to come heavily into play.

Would we honestly like perfect dogs engineered by geneticists? I think not, for certainly many famous and great Cavaliers of the past were far from perfect. It was their individuality, their uniqueness, their character, and that elusive star quality, which made them stand out. To try and study genetics, anyway, has most people reaching for the headache tablets in a very short time. Indeed stars are born and not engineered, for I believe there are no such people as lucky breeders – they make their own luck through their perseverance and dedication. To enjoy what you are doing is the best recipe for success.

TRADITIONS

Great Britain has never been short of natural stock men and women and the country has not earned the reputation of being the 'stock farm of the world' lightly. It comes from generations of successful animal husbandry, including dog-keeping, which has been handed down through the generations. Children learn the art from their talented, knowledgeable parents as they grow up and without really having to think about it. It becomes a part of everyday life, the daily feeding, exercising and grooming of the family's pets.

Here the Cavalier King Charles Spaniel enjoys the strongest gene pool and thrives like nowhere else, and, generally, the British know how to look after them. The breeders, in the main, are about as moderate as their climate in their approach to veterinary care, management and breeding programmes. Indeed, continents can change the physical appearance and Breed Type of different dogs, just by the traditional ways of keeping them, and of feeding methods and because of the climate and weather patterns. However, Britain, like any other country, has the undesirable minority of people who are 'right over the top' in their ideas and management. Indeed every year in this country somebody always manages to come up with a different ailment theme, with the guaranteed regularity of the Chinese New Year – but it is not so much the 'Year of the Monkey' as, say, the 'Year of the Retinal Folds'.

While it is a good idea to bring these things to the attention of the breeders for them to watch, some people positively thrive on looking for some flaw! Always they seem to be looking for veterinary perfection and, by the same token, some breeds have been ruined by introducing exaggerations on the breeder's part. If either extreme is persisted in, it may prove the downfall of the breed. Fortunately the established and most successful breeders are more long-sighted and tolerant with the stock. They know what it takes to produce the top dogs – years of hard work, expense and dedication. For these reasons common sense usually prevails in the end.

For every story behind every successful top dog there are guaranteed stories of heartbreak and bitter disappointments. The Cavalier King Charles Spaniel has never enjoyed such excellent all-round health as it does now, and "well done" to that vet who stood up and said there was not much wrong with the breed. Equally refreshing was the British Veterinary Association eye specialist who commented that the truly large eyes of the Cavalier rarely suffered problems, unlike the small, untypical eyes being bred in at an alarming rate. By keeping the eyes large, the breeders will stay out of trouble.

USING COMMON SENSE

Common sense is very cheap, in fact it costs nothing. If breeders would only use the outstanding senior dogs, instead of rushing out to use the latest young star, they would soon come to grips with the problem of longevity in the breed. By using the families which are noted for long life, heart trouble will eventually, with time, become a thing of the past, as have the other faults with which the early breeders had to contend.

In seeking to produce sound stock of the highest order, what must never be lost sight of is the Breed Type. It comes before anything else, and the breeder who places more store on clear medical certificates than in preserving exquisite Breed Type is unlikely to have many serious breeders take any interest in their kennel's stock in the long term.

BREED TYPE

Breed Type is one of the most difficult things to define. The quality and classical outline of the dog in question, its symmetry and balance, the air of a well-bred dog, its capacity to embody the many qualities and characteristics required by the Standard for that Breed are very much in the eye of the beholder. The true head is so important and, as has already been discussed, it used to count for over half the points which were awarded to the whole dog. Without being able to see the rest of the dog, just a glimpse of the head tells us how good its Breed Type and quality is, more so than being able to see just the body and the rear end of the dog. Excellent Breed Type should exclude everything that is vulgar, common, irregular and discordant in outline. It is the overall excellence and the presence of as many breed characteristics as possible in the individual dog, plus the correct temperament for that breed, which can earn it the description honestly as 'Excellent Breed Type'.

JUDGING

Judging should never be taken lightly. In fact a fair deal of responsibility for the favourable development and progression of the breed rests squarely on the judge's shoulders. One will never stop novices rushing off to use the class winners of the day, thinking that the judge is godlike and so that is what is required to win. For a new and inexperienced judge, the act of stepping into the middle of a show ring surrounded by a packed audience, waiting with anticipation, can feel like stepping off the edge of the world. Everybody can be excused a simple, innocent mistake when judging, with a slight difference of opinion, but what the majority of the crowd will expect is honesty. With so much time and expense concerning dog-breeding at stake, first impressions about a new judge usually last!

If the same exhibitor has the best dog in each class, then they should win every class. In each class the judge should be looking for the dog which fits the Standard the best with a view to awarding that dog top honours at the end of the class judging, regardless of who is holding the lead.

EXHIBITING

For the disappointed exhibitor there is always another show and there are many pairs of eyes watching in the audience that won't necessarily have agreed with the judge's decision – providing the breeder is not seeing their 'geese as swans': if they can see a few 'ifs' about their dog at home, then the knowledgeable judge will certainly spot those faults, and a few more. Years ago, if somebody had a dog good enough, nothing and nobody would stop that animal going to the top, and one would hope that is still true today.

In the last decade or so, the UK has seen a sad exodus of many judges of the highest calibre. They were the type who were just waiting for exhibitors to bring exciting dogs into the ring. They loved going over them, giving them high honours and priding themselves on spotting raw talent. Their reputations preceded them and it was an honour to win under those judges; it was not a case of how many CCs one won – it was who had awarded them to you. May this long be the case, along with the traditions of good sportsmanship and dog handling in the UK, where the long leads are legendary – and Cavalier exhibitors, particularly, would never dream of letting the rest of the class see them get down on their knees to their dogs, 'topping and tailing'.

SUCCESSFUL BREEDERS

As regards the breeders themselves, private research shows how few people come up with the random individual champion. It is the ones who acquire a bitch, sometimes not a spectacular one, and just get on with it, who make the best breeders. Studies reveal that the most successful ones practised careful line breeding to up-grade their stock, with the occasional outcross stud dog to bring in a desired quality which was lacking. The results are apparent in the lasting, and continually successful, production of good dogs.

'Red' pedigrees don't always guarantee the production of good dogs but, certainly, a good dog has to have the pedigree to match if other breeders are to take an interest in the line. A good specimen, without the pedigree to suggest it should be in existence, unfortunately earns the label of 'freak' or 'one-off'.

As the pedigree lengthens, the influence from the dogs in the background diminishes quickly, and it is the dogs in the previous three generations which must be studied closely. A breeder must get to know all they can about how they looked, their faults and temperament and, most important, what type and qualities they produced in their progeny. Remember, all Champions have faults but, hopefully, they were the best of their generation the year they were made up.The Golden Rules about breeding are: never breed two dogs together with identical faults, and double up on as many positive qualities as possible. When the breeder appraises a litter at eight to nine weeks, the end result must be closely examined to see if these first principles bore fruit. Never run anything on which is not at least as good as, and, hopefully, much better than, the dog before.

While researching this book it was not difficult to realise what a great lady Amice Pitt was, even if one had never met her. Her quotes are still very quotable and in 1978, fifty years on from the beginnings of the breed, she wrote: "Now we have one of the highest registrations, are we doing any better? I doubt it. We suffered then, and still do, from the complete ignorance of many interested people."

It is not easy keeping up the Standard of the first class Cavalier King Charles Spaniel – but it is a lot of fun trying! Amice Pitt is still the source of inspiration to many, and it just goes to show how one person can make all the difference. If this book inspires that one person, then it will have served its purpose.

Chapter Eleven

BREEDING CAVALIERS

THE BROOD BITCH – WRITTEN AND UNWRITTEN RULES

I consider that a brood bitch should be treated like a Queen, for the whelping box is where fortunes are won or lost. There was never a truer saying than the old adage: 'The strength of a kennel lies in its brood bitches'; and, by the same token, breeders who abuse their females deserve all the bad luck that usually comes to them in time.

It is true that many bitches positively thrive on having puppies whilst others simply hate the whole business, so the management of brood bitches lies very much within the conscience of the individual breeder and owner. When it comes to looking after these prized females no expense or effort should be spared. Fortunately the English Kennel Club has, in recent years, laid down firmer guidelines to be followed, which also act as a reminder to those people who are not too sure what they are supposed to be doing with their brood bitches! Furthermore the KC will no longer register litters whelped from a bitch over her eighth birthday or one who has had more than six litters in her lifetime.

How could she fail to be great? Stamped with the look of eagles, and the Champion's elbow markings, Molly Coaker's classical bitch, Ch. Homerbrent Samantha (born 25.8.1972) also bred three Champions. She was sired by Homerbrent Highlander out of Homerbrent Annadrewan.

Thomas Fall.

Peggy Talbot
holding Crufts Best
of Breed Ch.
Maxholt Christmas
Carol: the direct
result of mating a
black and tan and a
blenheim together.

The Cavalier King Charles Spaniel Club of Great Britain endorses the KC's rules by including in their Code of Ethics that the age-limit be eight years with, again, no more than six litters. Added to which, the Club stipulates to members that no bitch be allowed more than two Caesarian sections and that she must be at least sixteen months of age when producing her first litter. No bitch should normally rear a litter on consecutive seasons and, in any case, bitches must have no more than two litters in any two years.

In the USA their Cavalier King Charles Spaniel Club states no restrictions concerning Caesarian sections but agrees that no bitch is to rear more than six litters in her lifetime, and none beyond her eighth year. The bitch should not be bred before she is one year old and then only if she is sufficiently mature and in excellent health. The bitch is to whelp only two litters during three consecutive seasons.

THE IDEAL SUBJECT
The outcome of any successful mating is, by and large, chiefly due to the brood bitch herself.

The ideal female should have a calm, intelligent outlook on life and be neither aggressive, nor nervous in her temperament. She should be jolly, active, responsive and eager to please, which is preferable to the fat, lazy and dull bitch who is just content to lie around all day and lacks any real character and intelligence. Most important of all, there should be a real trust and rapport existing between dog and breeder, for this bond comes heavily into play when the whelping takes place and you are dealing together with all the problems that may come with it – a time when dog and owner may be very alone.

EARLY PREPARATION
The ideal brood bitch should be in excellent condition prior to mating. To attempt to breed a litter from one who isn't is just sheer folly and the owner is on a losing line straightaway. By excellent condition I mean bright, intelligent eyes and supple, firm body tone, being neither too fat nor too thin. The bitch should have lost her coat just prior to her season but, even so, the coat and skin should have a sleek, healthy appearance with a loose pelt.

An early checkover by the vet prior to the bitch coming into season is always advisable, to confirm her good health and readiness to bear a litter. Her heart should be sounded and a general inspection done to confirm she has no disease or abnormalities and, if she has to be wormed, now is the time to do it, well away from the season and pregnancy. The owner can supply a stool sample to ascertain whether worming is required, for indiscriminate worming can be just as harmful as the worms themselves.

If the stud dog owner requires a negative swab certificate, then the brood bitch owner should deal with this formality well before the bitch comes into season. Swabs can be taken half-way between seasons and, if anything untoward is discovered, then there is time for the bitch to be treated and re-tested prior to the mating. The potential brood bitch should, from puppyhood, have been raised and fed as described in the appropriate chapters, to ensure that she is in the pink of condition, with firm, moderate bone, and that she is a bright, sparkling and biddable individual.

THE SIGNS OF PREGNANCY
After the selection of a suitable stud dog and after the mating has gone according to plan, the owner/breeder then waits with eager anticipation for the happy event. Early signs that the brood bitch has held to the mating are shown almost immediately by the fact that her season ends abruptly, although sometimes her vulva still remains a little puffy in appearance. Her temperament goes very quiet and contented and her coat, which should be growing in fast now, should have an unmistakable bloom to it. A bitch never looks any better during her young life than when she is a few weeks pregnant.

At three weeks into the pregnancy the bitch many suddenly become finicky about her food, and this condition may last for a week while her hormones adjust. The owner should not be too concerned about this and can read it as a good sign, but certainly if the bitch continues without eating much, veterinary advice must be sought.

Some clever breeders are able to detect with their fingers at twenty-eight days whether there are any puppies present, and some breeders like their bitches to be scanned by the vet at a suitable time to try and determine if the bitch is in whelp, and how many. Obviously a bitch that is empty can still carry out her show engagements. It also helps to be forewarned about numbers as the whelping draws nearer, particularly if the bitch is carrying only one puppy. Some bitches with an excellent spring of rib can keep their owners guessing right up until the last couple of weeks, as the puppies can be carried high up and elude manual detection. At five weeks, though, the tell-tale signs of the nipples reddening and standing up, accompanied by the udder starting to form, is usually a sure sign of the pregnancy.

FEEDING THE PREGNANT BITCH

Some breeders make the huge mistake of feeding their pregnant bitches up to the hilt prior to whelping, thinking they have many mouths to feed. In fact the breeder feeds only the bitch. The bitch feeds the puppies! Indeed the bitch nurtures what puppies she is carrying by the reserves she has built up through the excellent condition and care her owner has lavished upon her prior to the breeding, as well as the fact that her discerning owner has afforded her lengthy rests between litters and is ever-mindful of her interests. This is highly preferable to a breeder trying to cram food into a thin, underconditioned and already pregnant brood bitch with the forlorn hope of making up the ground in the space of the nine-week pregnancy.

A pregnant bitch carrying an average litter of four should require little more than her normal rations, but what she is given to eat should be quality food, full of nourishment. Biscuits and 'all in one' meals are only 'fillers' and, since the aim is not to make the brood bitch fat and overloaded in the stomach, they should be avoided. The ideal food, to my mind, for a pregnant bitch is raw stewing beef, fed in small, diced pieces, for health and for stamina and to build the bitch up for the strenuous time ahead. According to the size of the bitch and that of her forthcoming litter, one would feed anything from six to ten ounces a day. Later, towards the end of the pregnancy, the main meal may be divided into two smaller ones, and a few nourishing biscuits can be fed. Additives in the food should be a few simple ones such as the dried herbs and garlic tablet daily. Raspberry leaf tablets are a well-known birth aid and are likely to achieve a clean whelping, where no afterbirth is retained. Vitamin E is a valuable additive to the bitch's diet before and after she has been mated. Bitches fed with this during pregnancy usually produce strong and lively puppies at birth, the sort that act like little pigs when they are born – after being popped out they make their way round to the 'milk bar' straight away! A good Vitamin and Mineral tablet is also recommended, and then the breeder has just about covered all eventualities.

The breeder should avoid adding too much Calcium to the food prior to the whelping. It is now a widespread belief that over-use of Calcium actually affects the bitch's muscle and uterus tone, the very thing she is relying on to see her through a safe delivery. A toy spaniel bitch should obtain everything she needs through a balanced, natural diet. The time to add Calcium to the food – and it is only necessary when the bitch is feeding a good-sized litter of, say, from four puppies upwards – is after she has whelped. The liquid-type Calcium supplement is more easily disguised in the food, and can be ordered through your vet. Good bone is hereditary and not fed. The bitch should be able to utilise the above diet very well.

At six weeks it may become evident, by her heavy appearance, that the brood bitch is expecting a large litter, so then, at this time, I supplement the food by splitting the main meal and also introducing a third meal made up of one cup of goat's milk and a breakfast cereal biscuit. Some bitches will not touch milk before they whelp, so other protein alternatives can be used, such as boiled egg, scrambled egg or egg custard. Cheese, chopped raw herring or pilchards are all satisfactory substitutes – but don't overdo it. Little and often is best. If the breeder knows only one or two puppies are present, then a normal dinner is quite adequate.

EXERCISE
As regards exercise, the bitch will like to pace herself towards the later stages but, if she is reluctant to do any at all, she can be taken on the lead for a short leisurely walk to keep her fit. Climbing stairs and jumping into and onto things should be avoided.

THE VET
The owner/breeder should make sure they are acquainted with a small-animal veterinary practice close by where they know they will receive efficient service should there be problems with the whelping, and it is a good idea to let the vet know when the bitch is due.

PREPARING FOR THE WHELPING
Cavalier King Charles Spaniel bitches usually go to their time of sixty-three days after mating, though some can be a couple of days early, so to stay on the safe side, it is best to start watching from the eighth week onwards. There are unusual cases where bitches have gone a week over time and still produced live puppies, but it must be stressed that this is very unusual and I would be a little concerned if one of mine had gone even a day over time. Often, if something has happened to one of the litter, the bitch will produce early, to get rid of a dead puppy out of her system and so save anything else happening to the others.

When it is obvious that the bitch is pregnant, she should become well accustomed to the area and the whelping box where the owner wants her to have her puppies. The diagram is of the type of whelping box I have always used. Two of them were made for me by a craftsman in Llandrinio in Powys over twenty years ago and, apart from the odd new piece of wood and a couple of screws for repairs, they are still in use. In fact I look on them as very lucky, memorable and valuable antiques, as some forty-four Champions have been born in them over the years. Fortunately Cavalier King Charles Spaniel bitches make wonderful mothers and are not in the habit of lying on their puppies, but they do like privacy. They do not resent their beloved master or mistress or, perhaps, another familiar assistant being present at the birth, but squealing, excitable children and strangers peering into the box will not only upset the bitch but also delay the birth. One owner present is best, with help nearby should an extra pair of hands be needed.

The whelping box is best positioned in a warm room, perhaps screened behind a settee and next to a radiator, with space for the attendant to get a comfortable armchair into the next corner and keep a discreet watch from behind an opened book or newspaper. If the breeder has been watching the bitch for a few days, then they usually have the box next to their bed, so that they can grab a few hours sleep and still be able to hear if anything starts happening. In any event the room should be quiet, warm and restful.

Laid out near to the box should be clean towels to dry and rub the puppies, a pair of sterilized surgical scissors, a reel of strong cotton thread, a nylon show lead made into a

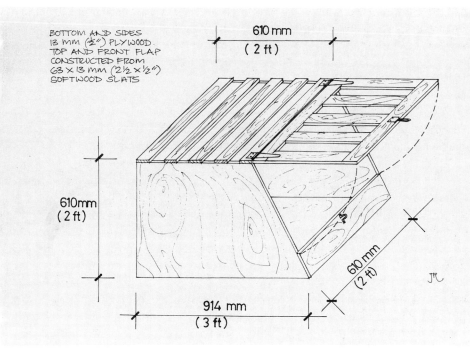

BOTTOM AND SIDES
13 mm (½") PLYWOOD.
TOP AND FRONT FLAP
CONSTRUCTED FROM
63 X 13 mm (2½ X ½")
SOFTWOOD SLATS

610 mm
(2 ft)

610mm
(2 ft)

610 mm
(2 ft)

914 mm
(3 ft)

Dimensions for the whelping box.

loop by passing the hand-piece back over the lead, or a clean piece of crepe bandage, a bottle of iodine to dress the umbilical cords, clean newspaper and spare bedding. A writing pad and pen to make notes and a watch or clock to keep a check on the proceedings are also required. If the bitch has to be taken to the vet with any difficulties, the breeder can then give a detailed report of what has gone on before. Last but by no means least, a small cardboard box should be made ready, with a hot water bottle complete with fluffy cover, and a hot-water kettle standing by. For reviving puppies in a hurry it is prudent to have already obtained from the vet some medication which he can prescribe, and to include this in the breeder's stand-by kit.

I give my bitches plenty of newspapers to rip up and an old double-bed sheet to whelp on. They have far more fun with these than with a boring piece of vetbed. Cavalier bitches are very enthusiastic mothers and, by the time they have finished making a nest, the resultant cloud of ripped paper and abstract jumble is quite admirable – usually with a happy, panting face with twinkling eyes in amongst it all! When the bitch gets close to her time the imminent whelping is heralded by her unusually strange behaviour. She may refuse her food twenty-four hours before, can be scratching up in her box for two days, or she may start excavations under the garden shed or in amongst tree roots. The specially designed whelping box comes in very handy at this time because, as the bitch becomes more erratic in her behaviour and can't make up her mind where she wants to be, she can be put in her box and encouraged to stay there by putting the lid down and half-draping it with a blanket to facilitate a private atmosphere.The certain sign that the bitch is about to start whelping is when her eyes display a little pain and show that she is now ill at ease with herself.

THE WHELPING
The whole whelping can be a nerve-wracking experience for the anxious owner, but the rest of this chapter is given as a general guide in those situations when the owner is really alone and the vet seems a long way away.

It is the owner who has the greatest opportunity to learn the most about what to do for the whelping bitch and it is a startling fact that not many vets have seen a whelping from start to finish. Usually the poor vet only sees the fraught owner and their bitch when she is in trouble, and then many vets admit that they agonise over when to intervene.

When the bitch starts to whelp she will have settled down in her box and, apart from the odd frantic scratching, whining or panting, she will begin the second stage of labour and the actual delivery of the puppies. If it is night-time, a well-placed light above the whelping box will ensure the owner can see what is going on from their viewing position – and from behind a book.

The advantage of using newspaper in the box is that the owner can make a check now and then by peering and feeling through the top bars, to discover if there are any wet patches. When these appear it means the bitch has definitely started. The owner then watches for the bitch to start straining, and this she does either by lying on her side or getting into a squatting position.

Her head will go up in the air and she will make a little 'wooing' noise while, at the same time, arching her back as she gives a push. The owner should be making notes about all this and watching the clock. When the first puppy is imminent, the contractions will be fluctuating between nine to four minutes, and will get closer still as the puppy is passed out. The actual contractions can start and go on for one or two hours, with longer intervals between, before these shorter periods are reached.

The first puppy is heralded by the appearance of a purple bag which appears on the outside of the vulva and looks very much like a large plum. If all is going well the first puppy should be arriving right behind it, say in ten minutes. One can only give a rough estimate of times but, personally, if no puppy arrives, I would wait no longer than an hour after seeing this bag, whether it becomes ruptured or not, to seek veterinary advice,

As the bitch strains hard she will let her owner know by a loud yelp or howl, that the first puppy has passed through the cervical opening and into the vulva passage. The surrounding skin swells up into a big bulge. This bulge is the puppy. Now the owner can go forward, open the box up and kneel down without the bitch being too bothered, for she will be too busy turning round rapidly trying to get to the passage. There is nothing better for the nervous owner than to get involved now and the bitch will be comforted and enthusiastic about such participation. The owner should steady the bitch and it is not a bad idea for the bitch to be wearing a light fitted collar for this purpose.

One more heave and the puppy should be born naturally. Not all puppies are born inside the placenta or afterbirth and, as they pass out of the bitch, the bags trail behind the puppies like parachutes.The most common way the puppy is presented is head first, with the head resting on the front paws, but breech births are still quite normal, and that is when the hind legs are presented first. With this type of birth it is imperative that the puppy is born as soon as the back legs and feet appear, or the puppy may drown because the head is trapped in the bag still inside the bitch. That is why the owner must get down and look to see what is happening and try to deal with the situation themselves. It is the wrong time to be loading the bitch into the car and heading for the vet's surgery if the birth is that far advanced.

If the head and shoulders are still jammed in the cervix opening inside but the owner can push back sufficient skin to expose the waist and back legs of the puppy, then something can be done. The best time to push the skin back is at the same moment as the bitch takes a heave. However, if the puppy is too high up and a forceps delivery looks likely, then a trip to the vet is inevitable. When attempting to deliver a breech puppy it is advisable not to try doing it with the bare hands, squeezing and pulling on the legs and body. Instead there are other ways, either by passing the looped show lead around the puppy's waist, with the lead passed through the back legs and the tie underneath, or by using a piece of crepe bandage, tied once, again with the knot underneath, secure but not strangling. When the bitch strains again, exert gentle pressure on the aids in a downward movement. This is where another assistant is invaluable, one whom the bitch knows and who can hold her head and neck quietly.

If the puppy can still not be removed with *gentle* pressure, then a clean vaselined finger, preferably with a short fingernail, should be slid up between the puppy's backline and the skin of the vulva. The average fingers should be long enough to be able to explore and to reach the chest and one front leg by locating the elbow. Push as far forward as is possible with the finger before bending it and locking on in front of the leg and chest. Then, with greater, safer pressure than can be exerted using the ties, the puppy can be drawn out behind the strong finger lock. All this should have taken place within minutes of the back toes first appearing, if a live puppy is hoped for.

If the head presents first but the puppy is big and rather jammed, the matter is not quite so urgent. Give the bitch a little time to bring the puppy herself, but do not delay too long as there may be others waiting to be born.

Push the vulva skin back behind the puppy's ears if possible and wipe the nostrils out with a clean tissue in case the exertion has started the puppy breathing. With the first two fingers held upside down, lock on behind the puppy's head, exert some gentle pressure when the bitch heaves and the puppy should slide out. Always verbally comfort and encourage the bitch, telling her what a good girl she is, and try not to show any anxiety.

Close supervision must be continued because, if the bitch turns quickly and bites the umbilical cord too close to the puppy's stomach, the puppy will then have a bad wound which can be fatal, through loss of blood and the trauma of having eventually to be sutured by the vet.

Some breeders might disagree about too much intervention in the birth, but to err on the safe side is my policy, and to leave nothing to chance. Personally I do everything for my bitches and they only just have to lie there and have the puppies!

If the puppy is out of the bitch, lying on the bedding, and the afterbirth is still inside the mother, grasp the cord as close to the bitch as possible using a towel, taking care not to pull the puppy by the stomach, and tug gently to bring the bag. The bitch must be restrained quietly but encouraged to lick the puppy to stimulate breathing. To avoid too much of a shock to the puppy, it is a good idea to leave the puppy and the afterbirth intact for a minute or two until satisfied that the puppy is vigorous, squalling and taking good breaths. Gentle rubbing with the towel stimulates and dries at the same time. Then, with the help of an assistant, remove the puppy from the box, closing the lid down to keep the bitch under control, and see to the cord in front of the box so the bitch can see her puppy is being attended to.

The supervision of the delivery and dealing with the cord help to ensure that the puppy does not develop an umbilical hernia. One person with a deft pair of hands is able to complete this important part of delivering puppies, but the assistant can hold the puppy upside down to keep the wriggling legs still while the cord is tied off flush to the stomach with a piece of strong cotton thread passed round and knotted firmly. The cotton ends are trimmed off and then the umbilical cord is cut, at a length where it is neither too short nor too long, so the bitch can grasp it and carry on biting it off. Do this with sterilised scissors and swab the cord stump with iodine to protect it and to discourage the bitch from worrying about it and making the cord bleed heavily.

Return the puppy to the mother and offer her the bag to eat. This will stimulate her milk flow. If she does not want it, dispose of it straightaway and keep the box tidy.

With one puppy delivered things should be going according to plan, particularly if there is no retained afterbirth. If the bag is accidently broken off and retained, it may be passed before the next puppy – but keep counting and making notes. The rest of the puppies ideally should follow at ten to twenty minute intervals and all this procedure will have to be repeated for each one. Some will be born enveloped in the placenta, which should be ruptured with the finger nails and taken off as soon as possible. Each puppy should be thoroughly rubbed and dried, making sure the open mouth and nostrils are free of fluid and membrane.

It is a good idea now to put the small cardboard box inside and at the front of the whelping box, complete with bedding and the filled hot water bottle. In it place all the puppies, bar the last one to be whelped. This should be left with the bitch to keep her occupied. The warm and dried puppies will not appreciate being soaked again by their brothers and sisters exploding on to the scene.

In between puppies being born, it is advantageous and necessary to get each of the older puppies up to the teats so that they can take some colostrum, the first milk, from the bitch. This very act produces the natural oxytocin in the bitch which keeps the strong contractions to produce the remainder of the litter. The milk will warm and comfort the mewling newborns and the bitch will be less agitated about them, while she concentrates on producing the remaining puppies.

With a bitch with only, say, three puppies in her, the gaps between births can be quite lengthy as each puppy works its way along the horns of the uterus, and the intervals can be as much as one to two hours without causing concern to the owner. The bitch may take short snatches of rest or even drop off to sleep but the strong contractions will wake her up at the right time as another puppy is imminent. She may appreciate a short trip outside to the garden but the owner would be wise to follow her discreetly, with a torch if it is dark, to make sure no puppies are dropped outside. The bitch may take a drink of milk with glucose, or glucose and water, if she has been panting a lot and whelping a large litter.

If the whelping is going well, it will be very apparent to the owner how important it was to have started off with a strong, correctly fed and conditioned bitch with an ideal character and temperament. Also, if the puppies are being passed easily, this means that they must be of an ideal size – roughly eight to ten ounces is average – through the bitch not being overfed.

Throughout the whelping it is imperative that the new-born puppies are kept very warm indeed and that is where the hot water bottle is invaluable because it dispenses with any need for a heating lamp, which tends to beat down on the bitch's head and make her even more uncomfortable than she is already. Any chilling to the puppies must be avoided at all cost or they will be lost. Keep a constant check to see if they are warm by feeling their bodies with the back of the fingers.

Some breeders prefer to use heating lamps and electrically heated pads underneath the bedding, but I have a dislike of both, for the bitch's sake. The brood bitch, during and after whelping, is already hot and bothered and the last thing she needs is to be heated up any further. Far better to have a warm area for the puppies to lie on and up against, and this they receive from a furry covered hot water bottle placed in front of the bitch and a little way from her. The newborn puppies can then commute between their hot water bottle and the other area where they are kept very warm – the bitch's body itself.

After the whelping has finished and the bitch has obviously no more puppies to come, all the bedding should be changed. I like using a deep bed of clean, opened-out newspapers with a proper bed blanket folded in four, so that each side can be changed and used before laundering. The bitch will probably scrabble the bedding about and arrange the puppies the way she wants them to be. After she has finished, the hot water bottle can be placed close to the puppies. Cavalier bitches are very intelligent and caring mothers and I have actually seen a bitch arrange her puppies and then take the blanket in her mouth and pull it over her precious babies to make sure they are cosy!

Many breeders prefer using the fleecy-lined vetbeds, but some bitches push them up in a heap and leave their puppies lying on a bare floor. When the bitch persistently does this, it is a good idea to sew a false back onto the vetbed with a plain piece of material, leaving one end open. A piece of hardboard can be cut to fit into this, like putting a pillow in a pillow case, so it will then be impossible for the bitch to scrape the bedding away.

I like the design of my whelping boxes very much because, after the box lid is closed and a thick blanket draped over the entire box to cover the slats, it becomes very cosy, warm and private for the family inside. I keep the hot water bottle replenished for a few days in the box, which I like to keep in a very warm room away from direct draughts. By the time the puppies are, hopefully, thriving after a couple of weeks, they should require little in the way of artificial heating.

WHEN THINGS GO WRONG

The first stage of labour reached by the pregnant bitch is the most worrying for the owner. It takes quite a lot of experience on the part of the breeder before they can recognise the subtle signs, good or bad, that they see in their bitch prior to whelping. If the bitch is near to her time, has done quite a lot of preparation by scratching her bed up for several days, and is now sitting there looking very worried and uneasy and doesn't appear to be doing anything, then it is time for some investigation.

As long as there has been no sign of wet patches on the newspaper or the appearance of the 'victoria plum', the bitch is still intact and there is no cause for alarm. All the same, a visit to the vet is advised, where an internal examination of the bitch will be made to ascertain whether the cervix opening is now fully dilated or still rather closed up. A good vet will be able to indicate to the owner how much more time should be allowed for the cervix to open up and may help the bitch to reach this stage with a calcium injection.

Many breeders learn how to make their own exploratory examinations with a very clean finger, and will often mimic what the vet has done. It is helpful, for example, to have felt a nose, or toes, presenting in the fully dilated cervix opening, if after some strong contractions by the bitch, a further examination reveals that the puppy has not moved at all. The breeder will then waste no more valuable time, and will be away to the vet with the bitch. On the other hand, if the cervix has not fully dilated and the breeder can feel nothing presenting, the breeder then is being a bit previous and can afford to wait a while longer, and check again a couple of hours later.

Cavalier breeders must also make it quite clear to their vet that Cavalier bitches do not usually go over their time and the last thing a very worried owner wants to hear is the vet saying: "Take her home...she will have them when she is ready!" A close rapport with one's vet is very important and saves a lot of harassment and bad feeling in the end. If the bitch goes home after the vet has seen her and continues to sit in her box with pain in her eyes without showing any signs of going into labour, then she must be taken straight back to the vet.

Probably, then, another internal examination will be made to see if the cervix is properly dilated. If the owner has not had the bitch previously scanned to ascertain how many puppies are in her, the vet will probably suggest a quick X-ray to find out how many puppies they are dealing with. If there are only one or two huge puppies, then it is senseless to expose the bitch to oxytocin injections to bring on contractions in a vain and dangerous attempt to make her bring the puppies naturally. Although it shortens the bitch's breeding life, and breeders like myself dislike surgery on their precious brood bitches, the best recourse for all concerned is a Caesarean section without delay.

Nowadays, with all the up-to-date anaesthetics and in-care facilities at the veterinary surgeries, including incubators for new-born puppies, the Caesarean section is not as dreaded as it was years ago. Of course special care must be taken of the bitch and the puppies, who must be kept very warm indeed and supervised onto the bitch's teats for feeding at regular intervals for several days. Usually, thanks to modern anaesthetics and their antidotes for the bitch and the puppies, the bitch is able to walk from the surgery to the car and back into the home where, with some encouragement, she should start looking after her new family. If after X-raying or scanning, the vet decides there are a number of puppies which are likely to be smaller, it will be suggested to the owner that, as the cervix is fully opened, it would be safe to now try an oxytocin injection to make the bitch commence strong contractions. The worried owner is now in the best place and the vet will usually wait to see one puppy safely delivered. Before the owner reaches home, however, another one may arrive in the car, and so it is a good idea to gather up all the stand-by kit, including the hot water bottle, before leaving home in the first place, and to put it in the car in case this emergency arises. A vet who trusts the owner might send them home with a syringe complete with oxytocin in measured doses, to avoid the owner and bitch taking another upsetting journey, if more is needed to keep the contractions going. But the vet usually asks to be kept informed by telephone and gives firm instructions as to the time intervals required before injecting the bitch again. Usually, once the bitch has got into a rhythm with her contractions and delivery, further doses can be unnecessary and harmful. A puppy should ideally be delivered after roughly twenty minutes of the bitch receiving oxytocin.

No two whelpings are the same and, indeed, a bitch can whelp a few puppies normally and still need a Caesarian section to deliver the rest!

If the breeder is unable to tell whether the bitch has whelped all her puppies, then the vet is the best person to turn to and, of course, many breeders and vets like to follow any internal examinations with a suitable course of antibiotics.

REVIVING 'DEAD' PUPPIES

If the brood bitch is giving birth at the veterinary surgery, then the animal nurses as well as the vet will be on hand to show the breeder how seemingly 'dead' or lifeless newly born puppies can be revived.

At home, where the breeder is supervising the birth, sometimes a puppy may emerge that looks already dead and is, in fact, very limp and lifeless. This puppy must be left intact with its afterbirth until strong breathing has commenced, but should be taken out of the bag and, with head held downwards, rubbed vigorously with the towel. The nose and mouth must be cleared of any liquid and membrane. The best way to do this is to shut the bitch back in the whelping box and attend to the puppy on a table.

The drops, prescribed by the vet, which the breeder should have standing by, should be dripped underneath the puppy's tongue. This drug sends a message to the puppy's brain to instruct it to breathe, and this should be achieved within minutes. The hot water bottle can be used not only to warm the puppy but as a bed for the puppy to lie on while being given repeated, purposeful and gentle strokes with the towel down the length of the body. It will also provide a cushion against over-enthusiasm by the breeder giving the other treatment which involves gentle, repeated pressing with the fingers on top of the heart area, located behind the left elbow and at the base of the ribs, with occasional stops to blow gently into the puppy's mouth, as in the kiss-of-life technique.

If the airways and mouth have been cleared then another technique can be tried. Hold the puppy in the right hand in a 'banana' shape. With the left hand closed slightly over the top of the puppy's head, direct the puppy's chin back on to its chest between the front legs, in a jabbing but gentle, purposeful manipulation. The head should be held well tucked in for one or two seconds and then released. After a few attempts the puppy should give a gasp, if it is ever going to. Some breeders keep up the heart massage and kiss-of-life technique for a while with some equally successful results.

The puppy when, hopefully, revived and taking good breaths, should be disconnected from the afterbirth, and when the cord has been tied and dressed, given back to the bitch for further stimulation by her licking and pushing the puppy with her nose.

Many puppies are born alive but, sadly, after being disconnected from the afterbirth, the very thing which has sustained their life up until this point, they breathe a few gasps and then stop breathing altogether. This condition is encountered in human babies where the part of the brain which governs the breathing has been damaged during the birth, or was non-existent in the first place, and the baby, on being disconnected from the placenta, is unable to sustain respiration on its own. As with puppies, they are usually hopeless cases.

If, after all these different attempts, the puppy still remains lifeless, the breeder can at least take comfort from the fact that they have given the situation their best shot, and it is best not to be too down-hearted. One should be just a little philosophical about the whole thing and accept that the puppy was just not meant to be!

Chapter Twelve

REARING A LITTER

THE FIRST DAYS

Cavalier King Charles Spaniel brood bitches, as I have said, make some of the best mothers when it comes to rearing puppies but, in very rare circumstances, they may not want to have anything to do with their newly-whelped litter. For instance, after too rapid and violent a birth, the brood bitch may refuse to get into the bed to nurse her puppies and can indeed show real aggression towards them.

The vet can do much to help the distraught owner by suggesting a mild sedative for the bitch plus a calcium injection. Within a few hours the bitch should jump into bed with her puppies and settle down to nursing them. Close observation of the bitch is most important, to check that she is not running a temperature or being made too hot by over-use of artificial heating. Her appetite should be good, except that it is prudent of the owner to keep her on a light diet for several days, particularly after probably devouring many afterbirths, which in themselves will nourish the bitch and encourage the milk flow. If the bitch does not look well at all there should be no delay in consulting the vet because the new-born litter are depending on her to help them through what is the most difficult couple of days of their lives. The most common thing that will affect the bitch adversely is any retained afterbirth.

Abundant milk is produced by correct feeding, and a bitch with a large litter, once she has got over the first couple of days, should ideally be fed as much as she requires, plus clean drinking water. Natural food, which is known to aid the bitch's milk production, is fresh milk itself, raw beef, cereals, particularly porridge oats, mashed cooked carrots in the meat feed, honey and raw eggs, plus the additives described in the feeding section, including seaweed, the green herb, and garlic. A good-quality crunchy all-in-one food can be left down all the time and the dishes of different things replenished as the bitch empties them. She will soon indicate which food she likes best. She must eat well to lactate well.

Those puppies which posed a bit of a problem at birth should be watched particularly and any which are wheezing or chesty should be ministered to. The homoeopathic remedies available from most chemists and health food shops for colds and breathing difficulties, are curative. The smallest puppies are easily treated with a little of the appropriate crushed tablet on the wet membranes of the mouth. Little and often, and a lot of perseverance by the owner, works wonders. But the two essentials required by all new-born puppies are warmth and food.

The sure sign that the puppies are thriving is the dramatic difference that takes place even in two days. The puppies may be born looking rather long and flat, with tails like shoe laces, but after several days the ones that are thriving take on positive features. The healthy puppy 'draws' itself up into a compact shape, the body looks well-filled, especially between the forelegs and around the stomach area. The coat is very glossy and sleek and the thin tail has filled up and now resembles the thick otter-like tail of the Labrador.

The owner should, several times daily, test all puppies for dehydration by pinching the fold of the loose pelt up in a ridge on the puppy's neck and back. If the ridge stays up in a hard, dry-feeling fold, the puppy is dehydrated and urgent steps must be taken to correct this immediately. Feeding must be supervised and, if the bitch has plenty of milk, these puppies must be held on to the teat and fed every hour until they look satisfactory. If the bitch's milk has not come down yet, steps must be taken to supplement the puppies' diet, using a dropper or a puppy's feeding bottle, with liquid supplied by the vet or recommended by the local pet store. I have always used two parts goat's milk to one part evaporated milk, slightly warmed, with a little pinch of glucose, and have reared puppies very satisfactorily on this. Weak and hopeless-looking puppies can be brought round with a little perseverance and there are many nutritional aids on the market, including drops and paste, which bring dramatic results within several hours.

Despite every care, during the first day or two it will become very apparent which puppies are not thriving. They will make no significant change in their appearance from when they were born. The legs and tail remain scrawny-looking, with a pinched, restricted look about the chest. The coat and skin look dry and uncomely and they are generally lethargic. If the owner and bitch are doing everything they can, then it is best to concede that there is something congenitally wrong with the puppy and it is just not meant to be. Quite a common ailment is that the puppy has a minute stomach valve or an abnormal rectum passage so, after appearing to start to feed all right, the body's functions are unable to work properly and the puppy dies shortly after birth. Small puppies can be reared but often become a delicate-looking adult and, of course, special homes are needed for them, where the new owner will accept them for what they are.

If the brood bitch is healthy and correctly fed she will take all the hard work from her owner of rearing and cleaning her litter. Apart from keeping the bitch fed and clean, and providing clean bedding, there is little to do to the puppies until weaning time.

Removal of the dewclaws and optional tail-docking by a competent person should take place at a few days old, and thereafter the puppies' other nails should be kept trimmed, removing only the white tips, so that they do not hurt the bitch when feeding from her. When stimulating the milk flow, the puppies will be seen to 'tread' the bitch's udder and jerk the teats with their mouths. When the milk starts to flow they will all lean back with rigid forelegs, and this is a good time to cheat a little if there are any weak puppies getting pushed out. The weak puppy can be placed on a stimulated teat that a stronger puppy has worked on to draw the milk and another, smaller teat found for the stronger puppy!

If, as the puppies grow and later in the lactation, if the bitch keeps jumping out of bed and is loath to stay with the puppies, this can either mean sharp nails or mastitis. If the latter is the cause she will look off-colour, be standing with an arched back and refusing her food.

Her udder will be hot and hard. The twenty-four hour cure is given in Chapter Thirteen: Health Care.

During lactation, and even if liquid Calcium is being given in the food daily, the bitch may still suffer Eclampsia, or Milk Fever. Failure to treat the bitch rapidly will result in her collapse and death. Never leave the bitch unattended for more than a few hours, because attacks are rapid and come without much warning. Early symptoms are continual yawning and shaking of the head. The bitch will start to sway and wobble as she is walking, which leads to complete collapse, with the head and legs held very rigid. These later stages can happen even while the owner is rushing the bitch to the vet, so there is no time for delay, day or night. Fortunately, after the vet has administered Calcium in the vein or under the skin, the recovery is just as rapid as the collapse. It is entirely at the owner's or vet's discretion whether the bitch will have any future litters, but of course the bitch has now shown a tendency and the owner should be on the alert.

THE FIRST FEW WEEKS

While the bitch is still nursing her litter, besides keeping their nails trimmed, the puppies must be wormed at three and six weeks of age. If puppies are orphaned for any reason, as long as they have received colostrum, it is not difficult to hand-rear them or find another bitch to take them. Some breeders, if they are able to match up the size of the puppies with another litter, might transfer some puppies to another bitch to relieve an over-burdened bitch. This transfer is best done when both mothers leave the room to go to the 'bathroom'. Then the puppies can be re-arranged, rubbing any new ones introduced to another litter with that bitch's used bedding to disguise the smell. But, if fed correctly, a bitch should be able to rear her own litter to weaning, whatever size the litter, with some ingenuity on the breeder's side if required.

A friend of mine frequently has fourteen or so puppies in her Rottweiler litters and rears them into well-grown, even litters. Her method is to split the litter in half, keeping some in a separate heated box and leaving the rest on the dam. She religiously gets up every two hours, night and day, and switches the 'shifts' around so that everybody gets a chance. She capitalises on the fact that she practises natural rearing, with plenty of raw meat and milk feeding, so her bitches lactate very well.

PUPPY ABNORMALITIES

Apart from the occasional squeak from the puppies and snoring from the bitch there should be total peace and tranquillity coming from the whelping box. Wailing puppies are usually cold, or hungry or have something wrong with them physically.

The breeder must examine the roofs of all the puppies' mouths to check there are no cleft palates. Any puppy found with one is not likely to thrive and is better put down by the vet.

Some puppies can appear to be thriving and feeding well, almost too well, but are still making a noise and appear quite tense when one picks them up. They are quite probably suffering from colic and there are several homoeopathic remedies, including chamomile, to ease this, as there are for any looseness in the stools. The professional person is best consulted.

The puppies' eyes usually open after about ten days and they start toddling around at three weeks. As the breeder sits and studies the litter they may notice any abnormalities in the puppies' limbs. One may be holding a hind leg out, rigid as a poker. This condition is seen in calves and nothing need be done about it. The leg usually comes into use on its own.

As the litter nears six weeks – though it may be noticed as early as three weeks – a puppy may be holding its head on one side, turning around in circles and seeming rather confused. This condition is water on the brain, or encephalitis and, again, stands a very good chance of righting itself in due course without any treatment .

Personally I have never had a 'swimmer' – that is, a puppy who, by quite late on in the weaning age, say six to seven weeks, has not started to walk. The limbs are held straight out from the body, which is usually very fat from no exertion, and the puppy is unable to put its legs down and rise to a stand position. I have heard of much success in obtaining a cure by the owner practising physiotherapy on the stricken puppy and manipulating the legs. In lambs and calves that are unable to stand I have had much success using the homoeopathic cure conium and have brought them to their feet after a few days and successfully reared them.

So, as has been shown, many seemingly disastrous situations can be turned around by a little perseverance and that magical ingredient, TLC – tender loving care. Indeed I can recall many occasions when I and my doggy friends have defied their own vet's opinions, including recommended euthanasia, and have brought about many success stories with their Cavalier King Charles Spaniels.

NATURAL REARING

When Gladys, the ninth Duchess of Marlborough, arranged for some floors in Blenheim Palace to be dug up to provide 'wild dog' conditions for her famous strain of Spaniels, she might possibly have been considered a little eccentric by some people's standards. But to my mind she sounds like a lady after my own heart, and photographs of her exquisite, quality dogs sitting against a backdrop of luxurious tapestries bear testimony to her eminent accomplishments as a dog breeder and confirm that her judgement was not addled.

Indeed American-born Gladys Deacon was a lady of some style and even her assistant Mrs Grylls, portrayed in a photograph holding up an exquisite prize-winning ruby, looks more like the manageress of a fine dress shop than a kennelmaid. But Gladys, who dazzled European society at the turn of the century, was noted for being unconventional. Legend has it that she had imitation chocolate 'doggie jobs' made which she left lying around on the carpets. She took delight in then watching the faces of her society guests as she scooped the suspicious looking objects up off the carpet and started to eat them.

Like any serious, far-sighted dog breeder, Gladys knew the importance of her dogs having direct contact with mother earth. Indeed any breeder who practises natural rearing, knows that access to open grassland, free running, and daily fresh air are of the essence in raising fine, healthy dogs and it is a depressing fact that many Cavaliers worldwide experience none of these on a regular basis. Those poor dogs, in time, are likely to have a predisposition to suffer from one or more of many complaints including obesity, ear canker, skin troubles, hysteria, wasting of the muscles as in muscular dystrophy and many other disorders.

A litter, pictured at ten weeks, by Homerbrent James Bond out of Ch. Homerbrent Tradition.

Incorrect feeding is also one of the biggest causes of these ailments and there has been, in the last few decades, a swing to convenience foods such as canned and dry, expanded meals and pellets. One wonders if many people have lost sight of the good old 'meaties and bickies' enjoyed by generations of dogs. Indeed my late mother was a stickler for it. She used to send me off on the corporation bus into Birmingham when I was ten years old to buy horse meat for my first dog, a Welsh Terrier. I still remember the sickly smell which pervaded the kitchen as it used to bubble away on the stove, and the time it used to take picking the creepy pieces of newspaper off the raw meat!

The simple fact of the matter is that dogs are carnivores, animals who in their natural state would eat only raw meat together with the green herbal contents of their victims' stomachs. Dog biscuits and processed meals are fine kept in reserve, but should only be used when the correct protein foodstuffs are unavailable; and canned meat comes in very handy when fresh meat is short. But as I have always said, if I didn't have access to a good supply of raw meat, I wouldn't attempt to breed dogs at all, although it is true that some breeders get very good results using canned and dried food and I wouldn't dare to criticise their methods.

But if incessant, expensive vet bills, continual and copious amounts of mess invading the kennel areas, and short-lived, infertile stock become the bane of the breeder's life, it is worth considering Natural Rearing. Naturally reared stock are noted for a higher resistance to disease, they are definitely more pleasant to clean up after and, most importantly, they have the distinct edge on other breeders' show dogs in looks and performance.

FEEDING PUPPIES

Little and often is the maxim for young weanlings and this can be undertaken from around three to four weeks of age when the puppies start toddling around and show a lot of interest in their mother's food dish. Indeed the bitch is a very good teacher and puppies soon collect around a flat, shallow dish to enjoy the same food. The best ingredients for the puppies to

A complete and level litter at eight weeks, all naturally reared, and very saleable in the late 1980s.

A litter of puppies, pictured in the 1940s, sired by Ch. Jupiter of Ttiweh out of Tasmin of Torlesse.

Susan Burgess, one of the great breeders, pictured with Crisdig Angelique as a puppy.

Ch. Salador Celtic Prince, owned and bred by Sheila Smith. He is still the youngest post-war Champion at twelve and a half months.

Diane Pearce.

take at first, to commence weaning, are the milk and cereal feeds. The dry puppy flake I like to give them is one which can be soaked just prior to feeding and can be made to a porridge consistency, readily eaten by puppies as young as three weeks of age, and it gives variety to their diet. To start pushing scraped, raw meat down a puppy's throat too soon is the best way I know to cause digestive disturbances and to introduce unwanted bacteria. However, a Cavalier puppy is quite capable of coping with finely minced raw beef at five weeks, which is the correct age at which to offer it.

Minced cooked chicken and rabbit combined with wholemeal puppy biscuit or pre-soaked barley flakes are all excellent, as is egg custard and scrambled egg if proper fresh milk is unavailable. Milk is a perfect food. Some puppies wean themselves off it entirely, but if my puppies like drinking it then I keep feeding it to as late an age as twelve months.

Goat's milk is magical stuff and famed for the firm, quality body and bone condition it imparts to young growing dogs. Indeed we have won Championships with dogs from the Puppy class, so advanced were they in coat and condition. I have a lot to thank a goat for, as, back in the early seventies, my mission to find a billy goat for my nanny goat brought me to the door of Pant Isa, in North Wales, the home of Sheila Halsall. I left not only a highly satisfied goat, but with my first Cavalier, Pantisa Christmas Carol!

All puppies should be weaned off the dam by no later than seven weeks, but Cavalier bitches need some patience over this from their owners, as they tend to want to stay with their puppies for much longer than many other breeds. Young puppies need at least four small meals, spaced at regular intervals during the day. By four months they should be on three meals, then reduced to two meals at six months. Some breeders and owners keep their dogs on two meals a day for life. It is just a matter of personal choice. It is as well to remember that a growing Cavalier puppy may need the same amount of food as a grown adult, but the total amount is split over more meals. They certainly can't exist on scraps!

ADULT DIETS

It is essential that show dogs and future breeding stock are fed correctly. For long term success, health and fertility, there is no better diet than the natural one. Indeed, it is easy to keep a show dog in perfect shape using meat, with the addition of wholemeal biscuit or barley flakes, to keep the exact amount of flesh on the body.

Meat comes in all varieties but the most popular one, used for generations by many British breeders, is the bland meat – green, raw tripe with the occasional addition of a little red meat and a small feed of cooked liver once a week. During the sunless months of winter, cod-liver oil and a little seaweed powder should be added, plus daily garlic, fed in pill or powder form. Cod-liver oil should be replaced with vegetable oil in summer months, and seaweed and maize products discontinued, as these additives will heat the dog up and cause scratching and skin problems. A teaspoon of wheatgerm, fed daily all year round, is invaluable, as is the green herb which can be obtained from canine herbalist companies.

Fresh drinking water should always be available, provided in metal, not plastic, bowls. Dogs with faulty pigmentation and poor coat and skin condition change dramatically after reverting to the Natural diet. Liquid nettle and blackberry additives can be added to the dinner for improving pigmentation, plus a daily dose of sepia for hormonal disturbances, which are sometimes the cause of off-coloured noses. But if Cavaliers are born with suspect pigmentation, special dietary additives are not likely to make any difference. Black nose pigmentation must be bred, for to mate a tricolour to a blenheim with faulty pigment only masks the problem. The solution lies in only breeding to rubies or blenheims with outstandingly good pigment – and these are usually bred from previous generations of excellently pigmented dogs.

OUTSIDE RUNS

There is nothing better than long, continual hours of hot, dry sunshine to improve nose pigment. If a breeder has long-term plans with dogs, then much expense and planning must be considered to provide safe outside runs of different types. Many breeders like gravel runs, to keep the hair on the Cavalier's feet under control. They are handy to turn dogs out into after a shower of rain, which quickly becomes absorbed. In wet weather, and for show dogs, many breeders construct covered areas protected by white, fine, wood shavings or sawdust, which are invaluable for exercising dogs who are freshly bathed and groomed, ready for a show. Slab and concrete runs are easy to keep clean and wear the dog's nails down naturally. And, in fine, dry weather, what better sight is there than to see Cavaliers racing and playing in a lovely enclosed grass paddock?

If the owner's pocket can stretch that far then the ideal is to have something of everything to meet the daily demands of the dog – whatever the weather!

Chapter Thirteen

HEALTH CARE

PILLS AND POTIONS

Modern-day dog owners have never had it so good when it is necessary to use the greatly advanced diagnostic and orthopaedic techniques of the veterinary surgeon. Just a simple blood or urine test these days can tell us so much about a dog's medical problems. But the Cavalier King Charles Spaniel, like so many other breeds, can be very sensitive when it comes to the use of hard drugs. If ever there was a breed which lends itself favourably to and, indeed, thrives upon, alternative medicine, be it herbal or homoeopathic, then it is the Cavalier.

For years I have had more than a passing interest in herbal medicine and, in the last few years, I have been very impressed by homoeopathic cures. I am a great admirer of Juliette de Bairacli Levy. She wrote *The Complete Herbal Handbook for the Dog,* published by Faber and Faber of London, and buying it is a small investment for such a return in wealth of knowledge. Her basic policies of Natural Rearing to promote disease-free stock, prevention rather than cure and a total aversion to anything in food and medicine which is unnatural, drug or chemical based, are very wise indeed. She gave me the confidence to look after my own dogs in a more intimate way and to recognise, and treat, non-life-threatening ailments, thus quelling the urge to rush off to the vet at the slightest problem. My dogs have been Naturally Reared since the beginning and the results speak for themselves. Veterinary surgeons, herbalists, homeopathics and acupuncturists – there is a place for them all, and if a dog owner can find a professional who encompasses all these interests, then they are indeed blessed. But remember, all owners are free to choose for themselves whatever is best for their own dog.

ABSCESSES

These can be found on any part of the body. Treat by bathing with the hottest water the dog can tolerate until all the bad matter is expressed. Dry and apply general wound powder. An abscess which won't heal up may have a foreign body driven in deeply and the vet may have to lance it.

ANAL GLANDS

Many breeders and dog owners learn from each other how to check and empty the anal glands as part of the regular grooming process, and this is best done when the dog is being bathed. The dog soon lets the owner know when the glands are inflamed and blocked, by howling out and swinging his head round, trying to grab and lick frantically at the infected tail root area. Veterinary treatment is essential when it becomes this serious. Dogs fed on a natural diet, with plenty of roughage and green herbs added to the daily food, are less likely to have a problem. Old dogs are more inclined to impacted anal glands, when the tissues and muscles are no longer well-toned.

BURNS AND SCALDS
Apply a spray of cold water immediately and liberally to the burn or scald for several minutes. It is unwise to apply anything else until a professional person has seen the dog, but meanwhile the area should be covered with a clean piece of linen.

COLITIS (Haemorrhagia) AND PARVO-VIRUS
The passing of very loose motions, consisting of partly blood-stained material or complete pools of blood, is a sight which never fails to strike dread and panic, even into the most experienced dog owner. The symptoms of Colitis can easily be confused with those of Parvo-virus, but there are subtle differences. If the owner lacks faith in their own judgement and the attack is a severe one, professional help must be sought immediately, be it day or night. With Colitis the dog is fairly normal and quite happy, but lacks any interest in food, which must be withheld anyway until the dog has recovered. Symptoms can be accompanied by frothy sickness. Water can be left down. The dog will retire to bed for most of the day and must be kept warm. Symptoms usually disappear after a day, and a light diet can be introduced until the motions return to normal.

With Parvo-virus, which is a serious disease, there is an unmistakable smell of rotting tomatoes. The dog looks in obvious distress. The eyes are the give-away, staring and glassy. The dog may sit or stand, just staring at the water-bowl without taking a drink. There is usually much passing of blood – unlike Colitis, where the dog may only evacuate once or twice and then cease. In both cases the inside of the lips and mouth are pale, cold and clammy.

Emergency Treatment For Colitis: Give Aconitum 30c, one dose, and then, in a few minutes, check that the colour and warmth has returned to the mouth membranes. Phosphorus 200c, one dose, usually works like a charm. It is important when administering homoeopathic tablets that they are not touched by hand or tainted in any way. The small tablets should be crushed between two teaspoons and deposited directly onto the wet membranes in the dog's mouth. After an attack of Colitis it is worth considering the food and environment the dog has experienced in the previous couple of days. Repeated attacks need professional investigation.

CONSTIPATION
Usually cured by one teaspoon of liquid paraffin. However, if a dog has gone more than a day without passing a motion, looks very uneasy, refuses to eat and slobbers at the mouth, a trip to the vet is essential. These symptoms usually indicate that the dog has a blockage,

either from eating its own blanket or through swallowing another foreign body which won't pass through the digestive system. This is a life-threatening condition if left unattended.

CUT FEET AND TORN OUT NAILS

Immerse foot in warm water, clean and dry carefully. Dust with veterinary wound powder; do not bandage the foot but cage-rest the dog on a clean blanket, lifting out regularly onto clean, soft grass until healed. Deep cuts may need suturing by the vet. Half torn out nails must be trimmed off carefully to avoid the dog catching the offending nail, which causes further pain. Give cage-rest and gentle, controlled exercise on clean, soft grass until the nail heals and grows back again. Don't discourage the dog from licking the wound.

DEPRAVED APPETITE

This is the eating of the dog's own or another's faeces. It is a most disgusting trait, often thought to stem from pack habits, learned especially in puppyhood where the bitch's natural instinct is to clean up after her litter. It has been noticed that this trait does run in families – the son or daughter is as bad as the mother. Dogs fed on natural diets, with access to grassland, are less likely to do it than dogs confined permanently to concrete runs and fed on unnatural food that contains too high a level of protein.

The best treatment is to feed hard-boiled eggs, complete with the shells, ground up into food if necessary, or add Sulphur. Combine this with a good daily routine. Study the times of the day when the dog evacuates and then clean up straight away, thereby removing temptation. Catching the dog in the act and demonstrating in no uncertain terms, but without any violence, that this is a very dirty way to behave can be a big deterrent, followed by word association and an almighty roar when the dog is thinking about doing it again.

DIARRHOEA

Withhold food but not water until the condition ceases. Large doses of garlic and honey are very beneficial. Give Arsen Alb 30c, several doses if necessary and, when the dog is back to normal, start a light diet of minced, cooked chicken and moistened barley flakes. As diarrhoea can be an underlying pointer to more serious complaints, persistent and prolonged attacks must be referred to a professional person. Don't just ignore it.

EAR CANKER

This is a complaint which is most uncommon in a dog which has a healthy life-style. Toxic matter building up inside the ear, due to unnatural food and a lack of regular exercise, is the chief cause. But it can also come from cohabiting with cats affected with mites, so it is important to treat the latter as well. For prevention and treatment of ear conditions of a long-term nature I cannot praise enough the product called Thornit. A pinch of this powder in the ears once a month, or as part of the regular grooming process, stops any problems arising. One or two applications into the ears while I was grooming customers' dogs with long-standing problems provided an instant cure. There is no necessity to clean and probe around in the ear because, after the application, the dog, with a shake of the head, expels all the wax, septic matter and dead mites, along with the powder into which they have been absorbed.

FOUL BREATH

Dogs fed on tinned or proprietary foods, which can cause digestive and toxic disturbances to the body, often have bad breath. This can also be caused by neglected teeth and diseased gums. It can be avoided by regular checks on the teeth and gums as part of the normal grooming process. Tartar deposits must be scraped gently away from the teeth with the correct instrument, which can be obtained from the grooming stalls at shows. Swab the gums and teeth with a large piece of cotton wool soaked with dental cleaning fluid, available from the chemist's. It is the type used by old people who are unable to brush their own teeth; it loosens the tartar and is very beneficial to sore gums. Our dogs seem to accept this method more readily than tooth brushes and paste.

A deep red line between the gum and the tooth means the dog has gingivitis, a gum disease which will eventually loosen the teeth unless the above regime is adopted. Heavily tartared teeth cause painful ulcers on the inside jowls, which fall over the teeth when the dog's mouth is closed. Loose teeth, and ones that have really deteriorated, are best removed by the vet under an anaesthetic. In the case of a show dog it is important that the vet and the owner have a discussion beforehand. It is a widely-held belief that rotten teeth do eventually lead to heart and kidney trouble. Tell-tale signs of teeth and gum problems involve the dog rubbing its mouth along the carpet and crying out, combined with drooling and a reluctance to eat food, especially hard dog biscuits.

FRACTURES, DISLOCATIONS AND SPRAINS

These are cases for the vet. The orthopaedic aspects of veterinary care in modern times are extremely advanced and dogs can recover from the most serious accidents virtually without showing a limp.

Give Comfrey daily in the food to aid healing of the bones and to encourage rapid recovery. Comfrey is obtainable from health shops in tablet form if the fresh herb is not available, but in England it is a very common plant found growing in ditches, hedgerows and at the roadside. The plant contains Allantoin, the substance which effects the cure, and is commonly called 'knit bone' by the gypsies.

A greyhound breeder I knew always had a huge clump of Comfrey growing by her kitchen door and it was used on the injured greyhounds returning from the racetrack. The complete leaf is secured around the sprained joint by cotton-sheet strips soaked in cold water, which obtains excellent results. This cure works equally well on humans.

HEART TROUBLE

First symptoms seen, usually in the older dog, are a reluctance to take exercise and short, laboured breathing. There may be a dry cough present but more specific signs are fainting fits and actual heart attacks. The professional person can do much to alleviate these symptoms. A natural diet, with plenty of fresh air and exercise to keep the dog supple and fit, go a long way in the life of a Cavalier, but one that is allowed to get fat and does not exercise may not be so lucky.

Many Cavalier King Charles Spaniel can develop a heart problem sometime in their life and therefore the logical answer would be to breed it out with selected outcrosses. But since all Cavaliers go back to the same few dogs this is not feasible, particularly as it was amongst those dogs that the trouble originated. The mode of inheritance is difficult, if not impossible, to follow, yet Ch. Daywell Roger emerges as our standard bearer. He lived to be an honourable twelve-year-old, a good age for any breed of dog. Indeed it is too easy to become sensitive over the early demise of Cavaliers, since there are many breeds of dogs which are old, or dead, at six to eight years. It is also interesting to note that a young Cavalier can be diagnosed with a heart murmur at an early age and still live into the teens. Yet another dog can be monitored clear all its life then suddenly develop heart trouble and die after a short illness.

As the breed has developed and advanced over the years there has been a vast catalogue of Cavaliers living into their teens and it is these statistics that the breeder should study, not the negative aspects. Present-day Cavaliers are the legacy left by previous generations. Everybody has, at some time or other, bred good and bad; no-one has been exempt, either then or now. So by this token all breeders should be more helpful towards each other by identifying and making use of the dogs and their families which are living to good ages – providing, that is, that they are truly typical Cavaliers, for it is just as useless to be breeding for sound hearts at the expense of breed type. Cavalier breeders have approached and surmounted many problems since the early days and, I am sure, will eventually overcome this one, which is probably the biggest problem of them all.

For Cavaliers approaching middle age and those with signs of heart murmur, make sure the dog is receiving Vitamin C and Copper, preferably in natural food, or check with the different Vitamin and Mineral supplements available. Also feed Garlic and Honey daily. Both are excellent heart tonics. Homoeopathic aids are a mixture of Cratageus IX, Cactus 6c, and Strophanthus IX – one daily dose.

HEAT STROKE

When heat stroke is suspected, and definitely if the dog has collapsed, remove the dog to the coolest place possible and cover with towels soaked in cold water. Packets of frozen peas applied to the body help to reduce body temperature. In fact, on very hot days many exhibitors take frozen food in cool boxes with them to dog shows as a safety measure if their breed is inclined to heat stroke. It is always best for a professional person to check the dog over, however minor the attack. Of course prevention is far better than cure, so never leave a dog unattended in a car on a hot day, even if the windows have been left open. Cars can become ovens in a very short time, even on a mildly sunny day.

At home, always make sure when siting wooden kennels and runs that they are provided with partial shade all day. Study the sun's movements before planning any construction. Protect the run with trees or a high solid fence so that, when the sun is at its hottest, at midday, and throughout the heat of the afternoon, it is behind these shade givers. If kennelled dogs have to be left for a short time, the doors and hatches must be firmly secured open, so that no dog ever runs in and becomes trapped in a hot kennel.

Old double-bed sheets make great sun canopies, secured by long pieces of string tied at the four corners and then fixed in such a way as to provide shade over the kennels and runs. Always have plenty of fresh, cold water down and only exercise the dogs in the cool of early morning and late evening. Encourage the dogs to lie down and rest during the hottest parts of the day. In extremely hot countries dogs nearly always have to be kept indoors in air-conditioning during the day.

HERNIAS

Umbilical hernias occur where the puppy was attached to the mother by the umbilical cord at birth. They can be caused by an over-indulgent bitch pulling away at them. If the hernia is soft and not too large it should be left alone and, if it does not affect the dog in any way, I advise prospective puppy buyers to this effect.

Inguinal hernias are located in the groin area at the top of the inside back legs and can be detected by standing the dog on its hind legs and feeling gently down both groins. This type of hernia is considered to be hereditary and a puppy of either sex with this fault should not be purchased for breeding plans. The hernia can prove dangerous in a whelping bitch, apart from the fact that she will pass the fault on to her progeny. Small hernias do become absorbed into the surrounding tissues as the young dog develops into an adult.

KENNEL COUGH

This is a highly infectious complaint, usually caught at dog shows or from other areas where groups of dogs mingle. The owner's attention is usually first alerted to this tiresome complaint in early morning when the dog is excited about going out for a run. The cough is sharp and rasping and may be accompanied by the dog bringing up white froth from the throat. It is most costly and difficult to treat satisfactorily and, despite medication, usually runs its own course. The responsible owner must keep any infected dog separate from any other canine company. Kennel cough can be most detrimental to very young puppies, elderly dogs and bitches in whelp in the early stages of pregnancy, so prevention is far better than cure.

The best line of defence is all-year vigilance and attention to the correct diet and housing to maintain all dogs in tip-top condition. Daily dosages of Garlic and Fenugreek tablets in the main meal build up resistance to disease and ward off infections. The homoeopathic Kennel Cough nosode seems highly satisfactory. Once the initial three-day dose is given, it is a matter of keeping a diary to remember to dose once a week for four weeks and then on a monthly basis, according to the vet's instructions.

LACK OF APPETITE

All healthy dogs refuse food from time to time to give their digestive systems a rest. Young males can be very tiresome about eating when they have other things on their minds! Dogs fed on high-protein canned and dried manufactured dog food refuse food on a more regular basis, because the digestive system becomes toxic and the appetite wanes. It is important that all dogs are able to run on open grassland to search out and eat Couch grass to enable them to clean out their systems. Inappetence usually precludes or accompanies illness and disease. A simple blood test will reveal if the dog has a liver malfunction.

The dog who has obviously nothing seriously amiss, but who just exists rather than lives and refuses food on a regular basis, is the one dealt with here. It is very important that this type of dog is never fed on the diet mentioned above, or given steroids or any other chemical appetite inducers. These will probably just make the dog eat like a maniac for several days and then cease, before falling back into a worse state than before.

The dog must be kept outside in good weather for as long as possible during daylight and encouraged to exercise. Access to grassland is very important. The owner must harden their heart and withhold food for twenty-four hours. Offer food to the dog once a day, always at the same time, preferably late afternoon. Offer no food before midday. If the dog refuses the food or eats only partially, take the food up and instead push a large rounded tablespoon of firm honey down the dog's throat.

Establish the following routine: in the morning give Denes herbal tablets, with double the recommended dose of Garlic plus Liver tablets plus Gastric tablets, all bound into a large tablespoon of firm honey, pushed down the back of the dog's throat making sure no pills are spat out.

Repeat this at midday.

In the late afternoon offer the corrective diet meal: for an adult male, six to eight ounces of oven-cooked fresh chicken or rabbit, only roasted enough to enable the meat to fall away from the bones which must, of course, not be fed. The meat is chopped quite small and bound tightly into a cupful of pure barley flakes, obtainable from health food shops, which have been presoaked with tepid fresh drinking water. Never use meat cubes or any meat gravies.

In the late evening repeat the pills and honey.

A dog with this problem needs the natural Biotin from lightly boiled liver, and a small handful twice a week is very beneficial. The improvement will be slow but sure and takes a great deal of patience and tenacity from the owner. A painfully thin and run-down dog will show optimum improvement within three months. A small bitch would need only four to six ounces of meat and half a breakfast cup of dry flakes before soaking.

The owners must be prepared to keep up the Natural feeding regime once the cure is established, or all the good work will have been for nothing.

MASTITIS

This occurs in nursing bitches and females experiencing a false pregnancy. It is caused chiefly by overproduction of milk and puppies neglecting to feed evenly from all teats, resulting in the mammary glands becoming inflamed and painful to touch. The afflicted bitch is seen frequently standing in the bed and jumping out of her puppies' reach. She stands hunched up and looks miserable.

It is usually treated by a dose of Phytolacca 200, but the most satisfactory cure is Dock leaves, which works like a charm. Gather enough clean, fresh Dock leaves and shred into pieces to fit and fill a milk saucepan. Gently press them down, adding cold water to two thirds full. Heat the pan without boiling the water, just until the bubbles rise to the surface. Remove from the heat immediately and fit the pan lid, then cover the whole pan with a cloth to avoid the steam escaping.

When the liquid has cooled, nurse the bitch upside down in the lap and apply the potion liberally, using a small flannel and swabbing the whole of the mammary glands. Allow the liquid to dry naturally and encourage the bitch to return to her puppies, employing the larger and greedier ones as the 'milkmaids' to draw the milk from the hardened teats. Normality usually returns with twenty-four hours. This cure also usually removes any hard lumps caused by rough puppies bunting the bitch. This cure works on many other species.

POISONS

When poisoning is suspected always take the dog to a vet immediately, whether it be day or night. Take with you any packaging or a sample of the poison to enable the vet to administer the correct antidote as quickly as possible. If the owner actually witnesses the dog eating poison, the emergency treatment is to administer a drench to force the dog to empty the contents of its stomach before the poison can be absorbed into the system. The easiest and quickest way is a tablespoon of common salt dissolved in a pint bottle of warm water drenched into the dog' throat until the stomach contents are vomited up. Then take the dog as quickly as possible to the vet.

PYOMETRA

The best way for me to describe this ailment, the symptoms of which include lack of appetite, loss of weight, high temperature, panting, uneasiness and a purulent yellow or pink discharge from the vagina, is to quote two experiences of my own.

An old Labrador bitch of mine developed severe pyometra when she was eleven years old, having just had a season. Her seasons worsened her condition anyway. My vet advised me to have her spayed without delay, pointing out that the operation was a serious one even in a young bitch and that mine was less likely to survive surgery the older she became. I allowed him to operate on her. He promised he would make a new dog of her and he did – she almost made it to seventeen years! She was the only dog I have ever had spayed.

The other experience was that of a young champion bitch who had visited an outside stud dog. Late on in her pregnancy an overwhelming infection caused her to abort and she developed a high temperature and severe pyometra. My vet wanted to operate immediately on the bitch and was sterilising the instruments and preparing for surgery. Vets don't necessarily distinguish between Champions and other females! I had very bad feelings about all of this and I can still see the incredulous faces now as I scooped up my bitch off the table and hurried out of the surgery. I didn't know what I was going to do at the time, but I wasn't going to do that.

I turned to Juliette de Bairacli Levy's book. Fortunately it was late summer and there was an abundance of wild rose hips in the field hedgerows, the ingredient of the specific cure for this ailment. A few drops of witch hazel is added to an infusion of crushed hips, which is administered twice daily using garlic and honey in place of food, as the fasting is an important part of the cure. The bitch's swollen uterus and horns full of purulent matter subsided, giving way gradually to a clear discharge instead of the vile one which had shown in the early symptoms. My vet was very impressed and asked what I had done – and we remained friends. My bitch, who had been so ill, became lively and well and the cure was completed in a few days. She not only bred a live litter after a rest, but the pyometra never returned. It was a cure that cost nothing and worked. There have also been many documented successes using homoeopathic remedies amongst other breeders. The reader can ponder about all this and choose for themselves.

RHEUMATISM AND ARTHRITIS

There are numerous things that the owner can do to alleviate the pain and misery caused to, mainly, the older dog through stiffness and lameness. Always make sure old dogs are kept dry and warm and that their beds are raised off the floor and out of the way of draughts. Bean bags are very comforting and therapeutic and allow old dogs to lie in the most comfortable position to suit them. The dog will choose for itself how much exercise to take, and at what speed. Rheas, Tox and Arnica is a good homoeopathic cure and, herbally, parsley and watercress, fed as a fresh herb minced into raw meat, or fed in tablet form, are effective. The herbal manufacturers supply these herbs dried and sell them in small plastic buckets and they are very beneficial fed in the daily food to all dogs of whatever age. Also feed Cod Liver Oil which is specially formulated for the complaint. There are two types of the oil available. Copper chains are also known to bring great relief to the afflicted dog.

RINGWORM

This is a fungus-type skin complaint seen mostly on cattle and horses, but which can also affect humans and dogs. It is treated by rubbing half a fresh lemon generously into the offending patches and beyond the outer ring into the healthy skin. One treatment is usually enough and the patch slowly disappears and becomes engulfed in new hair. To obtain a firmer resolution, this treatment can be backed up with various homoeopathic medicines.

SKIN AND COAT PROBLEMS

These include scurf, bald patches, general lack of coat and intense scratching. Dogs fed on a natural diet, who enjoy a happy outdoor life and receive regular baths and grooming present few problems. Garlic fed daily on the food is a very important additive and the skin and coat become very unattractive to parasites. Incorrect management is nearly always the root cause of skin problems, be it in proprietary foods, lack of grooming or fresh air and exercise.

Extreme hot weather can cause scratching, and the addition of chopped boiled nettles minced into the meat feed is very curative. Cod Liver Oil should be replaced with vegetable oil and omit seaweed or any maize-based cereal food during hot months. Brown wholemeal bread or dog biscuit, barley flakes or rice are the best choices. A knob of polyunsaturated margarine should be fed on the food daily as another alternative.

When parasites are suspected, bathing at regular intervals with an insecticide shampoo is recommended – and I add a dash of washing-up liquid. When the coat is dry and groomed out, stand the dog on a grooming table with the head facing away. Fill a slicker brush with flea, lice and mite powder, carefully turn it over and draw it backwards through the coat from tail root to the back of the ears. Refill the slicker if necessary, making a three to four inches wide band the complete length of the dog's spine. Dust inside the ears with Thornit.

Bedding must be either replaced and burned, and treat all the fixed fittings with suitable sprays and powder. Flea collars are very useful, fitted after the treatment, and last about four months. There are herbal ones, and other types, which incorporate a coat and skin conditioning strip. There are chemical dips if the owner needs a last resort. In extreme cases of itching and hair loss when the cause is suspected to be parasitic in nature, I used Ascabiol, more commonly known as Benzyl Benzoate. This is best done on a hot day or applied in front of the fire on a cold day. The dog is painted from nose tip to claw roots with the manufacturer's recommended dilution. A small flat paint brush or a small firm sponge can be used to apply the mixture. Dry thoroughly to avoid chilling the dog, without rubbing or using any material. Discourage any licking and avoid the eyes carefully when dressing the head. The solution does not hurt inside the ear flaps or channel or when applied to the genitals. It usually works like a charm: the dog and the skin soon calm down and new hair begins to appear in a few weeks. Follow up with regular shampooing and grooming at suitable intervals. Loss of hair can also be due to an inactive thyroid gland. A simple blood test will confirm this. The homoeopathic cure is Flor de Piedre 30c, Fucus 6x (seaweed/kelp origin), one daily dose of each.

SORE EYES

Really serious eye injuries involving foreign bodies embedded in the dog's eye are very much cases for the vet to treat. But most eye soreness, including minor puncture marks, respond to the following treatments: give complete cage rest in a darkened room with only regular excursions to the bathroom. Then there is no finer thing than plain cold tap water poured gently into the eye using a small milk jug or a large piece of cotton wool filled and squeezed out. The dog can be held firmly, sitting in front of the owner, by being wrapped in a large towel and held firmly under the chin. Cow's milk and cucumber juice are both excellent for irrigating the eye and taking away inflammation and irritation. Repeat several times a day. Fortunately the eye is one of the quickest healing organs in the body. A dog which persists in rubbing its face with its paws, crying out and being unable to settle, is telling the owner that something more serious is there, and professional help must be sought immediately. After treatment an 'Elizabethan collar' is sometimes a good thing to fit, to prevent the dog from continually rubbing the eyes, until the injury has healed.

STINGS

Cavaliers can never resist having a snap at a buzzing fly, but wasps and bees can pose a more serious problem. If a sting is suspected, examine the area in case the barb of the sting is still visible. Do not pull out with tweezers in case the barb breaks and is left in the dog's skin, but gently scrape sideways with, for example, the flat, blunt blade of a butter knife. Most good neutralising substances can usually be found in the home, such as brown vinegar, Bicarbonate of Soda or slices of raw onion. Human cream remedies from the chemist work just as well, but if the dog has been stung high in the mouth or down the throat, professional help must be sought straightaway.

TUMOURS

These are most often seen in the older dog. If you can feel your fingers meet at the back of the tumour under the skin, then the tumour is usually harmless and is best left alone, unless it is too big, unsightly and impeding the dog in some way. Any lumps which cannot be isolated with the fingers and seem to be part of the dog, should be examined by the vet. Those which are felt down the side of the neck in a line below the ears, under the arm pits, under the belly and down the inside of the hind legs are usually ominous. Surgery will only accelerate this condition and cause the dog unnecessary suffering. Better for the dog to live out what time is left in a comfortable state, but euthanasia must eventually be considered at the right time.

WARTS

These, again, are chiefly seen in older dogs and can be unsightly and a nuisance when they bleed through being knocked. The old fashioned gypsy remedy is very effective and avoids surgery. Take the dog for a walk several times a day so that the owner can break fresh stalks from flowering Dandelions when they are in season. Immediately apply the white juice seen at the break directly to the wart. Use several stalks until the wart is completely smothered. This remedy can be safely used on eye lids and on the underside ear leathers. After a few days treatment the wart turns black and eventually falls away from the dog. Warts with 'waists' or stalks can, after several days, be tied off, tightly flush with the clean skin, with strong cotton thread for a more resolute solution, and they will soon fall off. Dab the root base for several days more with the dandelion juice and make sure the wart does not return to the same spot again. When dandelions are out of season there are tinctures and medicines available from the homoeopath.

WORMS

In England the only worms known to the dog are roundworm, tapeworm and wireworm. Outside Europe one finds hookworm and heartworm. Constant worming of dogs, sometimes unnecessary, can actually be more harmful than the worms themselves. A simple examination of the dog's stool under a microscope by the vet will reveal if there are worms present and identify the species.

However, it has been my experience and that of many other breeders that adults and puppies that have received garlic daily on the food over a long period of time eventually become worm free. We have indeed frequently had litters of puppies that, when we came to dose by routine with Coopane, were entirely worm free. Their mothers did not receive any conventional worming treatment either.

In breeding establishments where large numbers of dogs are kept on the same area year after year, there is always a risk of high worm counts and then it becomes a question of environment and management. Grass and gravel runs should be rested at some time during the year. This is best done in winter when, because of the bad weather, they are not being used a lot. A good dressing of lime is recommended, but always make sure every little particle has been washed in by the rain before turning the dogs out again for a run.

Every effort should be made to remove and dispose of all faeces, so affected dogs cannot contaminate the runs. There is a popular belief, usually amongst novice pet owners, that a dog seen scooting along dragging its posterior over the ground is a sure sign of worms, when it is nearly always a simple case of a rogue hair tickling the dog!

REASSURANCE

After reading this chapter through, the new Cavalier owner might be wondering what he or she has let themselves in for. These most common ailments met with by the dog owner are listed and taken from many years of experiences. The Cavalier King Charles Spaniel is usually a healthy, robust and clean little dog and that is why they are so popular and make such wonderful pets to own.

In Britain homeopathic remedies are available from pharmacists and health food shops. In the USA such remedies are available from similar outlets. In case of difficulty, see appendix for list of suppliers.

APPENDIX

BREED CLUBS

BRITAIN AND IRELAND
THE CAVALIER KING CHARLES SPANIEL CLUB
Mrs Lesley Jupp, 60 Roundway, Copped Hall, Camberley, Surrey
Telephone 01276 683282
THREE COUNTIES PEKINGESE AND CAVALIER SOCIETY
Mrs S. Jones, 7 Wellesbourne Road, Coventry CV5 7HG
Telkephone 01203 462816
SCOTTISH CAVALIER KING CHARLES SPANIEL CLUB
Mrs Morag Donaldson, The Bungalow, Langlees Farm, By Newmills Fife KY12 8HA
Telephone 01383 880336
CAVALIER KING CHARLES SPANIEL CLUB OF IRELAND
Mrs Evelyn Hurley, 14 Grange Park View, Raheny, Dublin 5 Eire.
Telephone Dublin 481621
WEST OF ENGLAND CAVALIER KING CHARLES SPANIEL CLUB
Mr J. Evans, The Sheiling, Gloucester Road, Standish, Glos. GL10 3DN
Telephone 0145 382 2599
NOTHERN CAVALIER KING CHARLES SPANIEL SOCIETY
Miss B. M. Henshaw, The Orchard, Wharf Lane, Sedgwick, Kendal, Cumbria LA8 0JW
Telephone 0153 95 60360
MIDLAND CAVALIER KING CHARLES SPANIEL CLUB
Mrs Mary Rees, "Little Oaks", 114 Hawkes Mill Lane, Coventry CV5 9FN
Telephone 01203 403583
EASTERN COUNTIES CAVALIER KING CHARLES SPANIEL SOCIETY
Ms Maryann Hogan, 1 Foster Close, Old Stevenage, Herts. SGl 4SA
Telephone 01438 317071
THE NORTHERN IRELAND CAVALIER KING CHARLES SPANIEL CLUB
Miss M. E. Elliott, 8 Glengariff Park, Bangor, Co. Down N.Ireland BT20 4UY
Telephone 01247 463166
SOUTHERN CAVALIER KING CHARLES SPANIEL CLUB
Miss M. Morrison, 3 St. Wilfred's Road, Broadwater, Worthing, W. Sussex BN14 8BA
Telephone 01903 230939

THE SOUTH AND WEST WALES CAVALIER KING CHARLES SPANIEL CLUB
Mr. A. Close, "Lamont", Claude Road West, Barry, S. Glamorgan CF6 8JG
Telephone 01446 737733
HUMBERSIDE CAVALIER KING CHARLES SPANIEL CLUB
Mrs Diane Jenkins, Churrasco House, Noel Avenue, Oakham, Leics. LE15 6SQ Telephone
01572 723116

UNITED STATES OF AMERICA
CAVALIER KING CHARLES SPANIEL CLUB USA INC.
Membership Chairman: Julie Starr, 105 East Monroe Street, Alexandria, Indiana 46001
Telephone (317) 724-7353
Secretary: Jacqueline Farrell, 1100 Deergrove Drive, Cedar Park, Texas 78613 Telephone:
(512) 335-8822

HOMEOPATHIC SUPPLIERS IN THE USA

Boiron/Borneman
1208 Amosland Road,
Norwood Pa 19074
(800) 258 8823

Doliser
3014 Rigel Avenue
Las Vegas, NV 89102
(800) 824 8455

Standard Homeopathic Co..
154 West 131st Street,
Los Angeles, CA 90061
(800) 624 9659

Washington Homeopathic Products
4914 del ray Avenue,
Bethesda MD 20814
(800) 3361695